WORSHIP

WORSHIP

Rediscovering the Missing Jewel

RONALD ALLEN
GORDON BORROR

FAMILY
CHRISTIAN
PRESS

WORSHIP
Published by Multnomah Publishers, Inc.

©1982 by Multnomah Publishers, Inc.
International Standard Book Number: 0-88070-140-4
Special FCP Edition: 1-893065-32-4

Cover photograph by J.P. Fruchet/FPG Stock
Cover designed by Mark Mickel

Printed in the United States of America

Unless otherwise identified, Scripture quotations are from the *New American Standard Bible*, copyright The Lockman Foundation 1960, 1961, 1962, 1963, 1968, 1971, 1973, 1977. Used by permission.

Scripture quotations marked NIV are from the *Holy Bible: New International Version*, copyright 1978 by the New York International Bible Society. Used by permission of Zondervan Bible Publishers.

Scripture quotations marked NKJV are from the *New King James Version*. Copyright 1979, 1980, 1982, thomas Nelson, Inc., Publishers.

Scripture quotations marked NEB are from the *New English Bible*, the Delegates of the Oxford University Press and the Syndics of the Cambridge University Press 1961, 1970.

FOR INFORMATION:
MULTNOMAH PUBLISHERS, INC.
POST OFFICE BOX 1720
SISTERS, OREGON 97759

99 00 01 02 03 04 — 7 6 5 4 3 2 1

To our wives,

Beverly Jean Allen
and
S. Janine Borror,

loving companions in the
adoration of God

Preface

"Worship is the missing jewel of the evangelical Church." The situation seems not to have changed appreciably since these words were first stated by A. W. Tozer.[1] Yet there is a significant change. The jewel is still missing, but at least now many of us know it, and miss it, and want to find it.

Evangelicals are now more and more aware of what we lack in worship when we gather together. The irony is even clearer. Evangelicals ought to excel in the worship of God. How can we who know God, not worship Him!

In evangelical churches across North America, one finds new committees or task forces involved in intense discussion. These are worship commissions. These groups are often excited with possibilities, but frustrated because of two factors: (1) They are not quite certain where they are going, and (2) they are not confident who will go with them.

Gradually some of the facets of the missing jewel begin to sparkle off in the darkness:

—there is a rediscovery of liturgy,
—there is an enhancement of community,
—there is an atmosphere of celebration,
—there is a new appreciation of environment,
—there are new ideas in participation.

Then even more startling facets of the jewel of worship are coming into focus:

—worship is declaring God's worth,
—worship is admiring God's character and delighting in His works,
—worship is God's plan for us,

7

—worship is a matter of art and of the heart.

Our book is designed further to recover the missing jewel of worship and to give it its rightful setting—in the local church.

Books on worship are sometimes written by church musicians or pastor/theologians. On occasion they are even written by a pastor's wife. Our book is written by a church musician, referred to as Gordon, and an Old Testament theologian, referred to as Ron. We believe this combination is distinctive. We have learned from each other (and have remained friends in the process).

Scripture quotations, not otherwise identified, are from the *New American Standard Bible* (NASB). We have taken the liberty, however, in some quotations to change LORD to *Yahweh*, the Hebrew name for God. This change is also done at times in quotations from the *New International Version* (NIV). Some Scripture renderings are our own.

We shall not forget Tammy Alsup who kept typing—and smiling!—for many days.

Our desire in this book is that our own worship of the living God—and that of our readers—will attest to the fact that the jewel of worship can be found and held aloft in evangelical churches.

Ronald Barclay Allen
Gordon Lamar Borror

Preface, Note

[1]Two decades ago Dr. A. W. Tozer preached a series of sermons on worship to the pastors of the Associated Gospel Churches of Canada. These messages from 1961 were then edited and published in a booklet entitled: *Worship: The Missing Jewel of the Evangelical Church* (Harrisburg, Pa.: Christian Publications, Inc., [n.d.]), p. 1.

Foreword

In his wisdom Solomon observed:

"Of making many books there is no end . . ."

(Ecclesiastes 12:12 NIV)

He must have been talking about *today*. Upon seeing a new book, one is often inclined to ask, "Do we really need another book on that subject?"

In the case of this book, quite a different question seems appropriate: "What took you so long?" There is definitely a need for this book. And there are good reasons to be so convinced.

We who are identified with evangelical Christianity are hard put to demonstrate any serious concern for worship in this century. As scholars we have failed to study worship, or give attention to the theology of worship. Principles of biblical worship are not sought as the foundation of local church practice. Most of our evangelical seminaries have not even offered full courses in worship.

It follows that as pastors, we evangelicals have not been much concerned with worship either. In many of our circles the Sunday morning event is considered a "preaching service" in spite of the fact that the official title in the bulletin reads "Morning Worship." Viewing the preacher's singular act of proclamation as significantly more important than the entire congregation's acts of adoration, praise, confession, thanksgiving, and dedication, is espousing an expensive heresy which may well be robbing many a church of its spiritual assets. And we have been zealous to reach the world for Christ to build up the body of Christ, while at the same time being negligent in giving our first, best love to God

Himself—which is what worship is essentially about.

As pastors and as churches we evangelicals have not taken worship very seriously.

But there are fresh winds blowing. Renewal in worship is beginning to sweep across the nation. The Holy Spirit is creating a hunger for God in the souls of weary saints. Believers everywhere are losing interest in merely going through the motions at church. People want to know God more deeply and to learn to worship Him more fully and to enjoy the priceless privilege of fellowship with Him.

The time is right for this book. And it is significant that this volume brings together the special insights and understandings of the scholar/theologian and the artist/musician. The authors have rightly assessed the need for a comprehensive approach to the subject—an approach which extends from biblical and theological foundations to the most practical of considerations.

When we begin to take worship seriously there arises within us very shortly a new concern for such matters as integrity, spirituality, emotion, intelligence, theological soundness, artistic character, balance, excellence, motivation, corporate action, architecture, symbol, gesture, order, spontaneity, acoustics, and a myriad of other considerations which relate to worship and worship services. Why do these become important? After discovering that our worshiping relationship with God is of highest priority, we find we must do everything possible to protect the reality of that priceless time with God. That includes the above concerns, and more, dealt with in the pages of this book.

The worship of God is the most blessed of all earthly vocations. There is no higher or nobler task to which we can give our energies and devote our time. God is first. God is worthy. And we are privileged to enjoy personal fellowship with Him. May this book be used by the Holy Spirit to help you more completely to love God with all your heart, soul, strength, and mind as you learn to worship Him in spirit and in truth.

Bruce H. Leafblad
Associate Professor of Church Music and Worship
Bethel College and Seminary

Contents

Part 1

The Definition of Worship

Chapter 1

The Essence of Worship

"Te Deum" *

Ponder the phrase *worship service*. Is your reaction "Oh, that's Sunday morning at eleven"? Perhaps for some people the phrase worship service serves only as a means to distinguish the Sunday morning service from the Sunday evening Gospel Hour and from the Wednesday evening Prayer Meeting.

But what do you think when you see or hear that phrase? Maybe your mind presents images of a lofty building with transcendent structure, muted organ tones, soft lighting, and of humble people kneeling quietly and communing reverently with God. For others, the words worship service might lead to thoughts of a storefront church filled with rollicking music, rhythmically swaying bodies, with smiles and laughs and shouts and luster.

Does the word *worship* make you think of robed priests with incense and candles, of color and ceremony? Or does worship suggest a wayside chapel on a country road having a battered sign: A Place for Prayer? Does worship make you think of preaching or communion? Of singing or praying? Of praising or meditating?

The word worship is used by many Christians for a wide variety of experiences and impressions. It is not surprising that the

---

*"(Praise) To God"

phrase worship service is used in several ways as well.

A RESPONSE TO GOD

Whatever else the word worship suggests to you in your own experience and expression, this word should speak paramountly about one's responses to God. While we do not wish to bring artificial limitations to the use of the word worship by believers today, we do object to its use in the phrase worship service if in that service there is no real opportunity truly to worship God. A worship service does not happen merely because a certain time period in the church schedule of events is so labeled. It is likely that we have all been in worship services where, by appearance at least, there seemed to be little true worshiping of God.

What, then, is worship? *Worship is an active response to God whereby we declare His worth.* Worship is not passive, but is participative. Worship is not simply a mood; it is a response. Worship is not just a feeling; it is a declaration.

Sometimes seminary-trained preachers bedazzle and benumb a congregation with repeated emphasis on the meanings of Hebrew and Greek words "in the original text," acting as evangelical priests with new substitutes for Latin barriers which only they may breach. But on occasion the English words we use are of surpassing worth and it is they that should be explained. So it is with the term worship.

DECLARE HIS WORTH

The English word worship is wonderfully expressive of the act that it describes. This term comes from the Anglo-Saxon *weorthscipe,* which then was modified to *worthship,* and finally to *worship.* Worship means "to attribute worth" to something or someone. When we say of someone that "he worships his money" or that "she worships her children," we are using the word a bit loosely. If, however, the supreme worth for him is in his money, or the highest value for her is in her children, then it is an accurate use of the term.

In Great Britain, the honorific title used to describe the leading citizen of a town is, "His Worship the Mayor." In the States we have changed this phrase to "His Honor the Mayor." To worship someone or something is to attribute supreme worth or to declare supreme value to that one or that thing. Along this line, Ralph P. Martin writes,

> If we may elevate this thought to the realm of divine-human relationships, we have a working definition of the term worship ready-made for us. *To worship God is to ascribe to Him supreme worth,* for He alone is worthy.[1]

HE IS WORTHY

Because of who God is and what He does, we attribute to Him the glory that is due His name. Such is the strong sentiment of Psalm 96:7-8.

> *Ascribe to Yahweh, O families of nations,*
> *ascribe to Yahweh glory and strength.*
> *Ascribe to Yahweh the glory due his name;*
> *bring an offering and come into his courts.*
>
> (Psalm 96:7-8, NIV)

We worship God when we ascribe to Him the glory that is due His name. This Old Testament hymnic text of Psalm 96 is balanced by a New Testament hymnic passage of great worship of the Living Christ, the Lamb Who is worthy:

> *Worthy is the Lamb that was slain*
> *   to receive power*
> *   and riches*
> *   and wisdom*
> *   and might*
> *   and honor*
> *   and glory*
> *   and blessing.*   (Revelation 5:12)

The triune God, the Supreme Being of the Scriptures, the Most Blessed One, Father, Son, and Holy Spirit—to Him worship is due from all creatures for all time.

> Father, we adore You!
> Lord Jesus, we love You!
> Holy Spirit, we honor You!
> We worship You by declaring Your inherent worth.

CELEBRATE HIM

What, then, is the essence of worship? It is the celebration of God! When we worship God, *we celebrate Him:* We extol Him, we sound His praises, we boast in Him.

Worship is not the casual chatter that occasionally drowns out the organ prelude; we celebrate God when we allow the prelude to attune our hearts to the glory of God by the means of the music.

Worship is not the mumbling of prayers or the mouthing of hymns with little thought and less heart; we celebrate God when we join together earnestly in prayer and intensely in song.

Worship is not self-aggrandizing words or boring clichés when one is asked to give a testimony; we celebrate God when we boast in His name to the good of His people.

Worship is not irrelevant thoughts or fragmented elements, silly asides or unconnected directions in purpose; we celebrate God when all of the parts of the service fit together and work to a common end.

Worship is not grudging gifts or compulsory service; we celebrate God when we give to Him hilariously and serve Him with integrity.

Worship is not haphazard music done poorly, not even great music done merely as a performance; we celebrate God when we enjoy and participate in music to His glory.

Worship is not a distracted endurance of the sermon; we celebrate God as we hear His Word gladly and seek to be conformed by it more and more to the image of our Savior.

Worship is not a sermon that is poorly prepared and carelessly delivered; we celebrate God when we honor His Word with our words, by His Spirit.

Worship is not the hurried motions of a "tacked-on" Lord's Table; we celebrate God pre-eminently when we fellowship gratefully at the ceremonial meal that speaks so centrally of our faith in the Christ Who died for us, Who rose again on our behalf, and Who is to return for our good.

As a thoughtful gift is a celebration of a birthday, as a special evening out is a celebration of an anniversary, as a warm eulogy is a celebration of a life, as a sexual embrace is a celebration of a marriage—*so a worship service is a celebration of God.*

One of the grand calls for celebrative worship within the Book of Psalms is found in the words of Psalm 100. In the words of the "old one-hundredth" we find a strong encouragement for celebration in our own worship. Here are these words:

> *Shout joyfully to Yahweh, all the earth.*
> *Serve Yahweh with gladness;*
> *Come before Him with joyful singing.*
>
> *Know that Yahweh Himself is God;*
> *It is He who has made us,*
>   *and His we are;*
> *We are His people*
>   *and the sheep of His pasture.*
>
> *Enter His gates with thanksgiving,*
> *And His courts with praise.*
> *Give thanks to Him; bless His name.*
> *For Yahweh is good;*
> *His lovingkindness is everlasting,*
> *And His faithfulness to all generations.*
>
> (NASB, with marginal reading at verse 3)

In our services devoted to the worship of the Living God and His Christ, let us celebrate our God!

Chapter 1, Notes

[1]Ralph P. Martin, *Worship in the Early Church*, rev. ed. (Grand Rapids: Eerdmans, 1974), p. 10. Robert E. Webber writes, "Worship gives expression to the relationship which exists between God and His people." Robert E. Webber, *Common Roots: A Call to Evangelical Maturity*. (Grand Rapids: Zondervan, 1978), p. 78.

Chapter 2

Art and Heart in Worship

*"O Worship the King, All Glorious Above,
And Gratefully Sing His Power and His Love"*

*T*here are myriads of electronic devices and gadgets available today. Whether you are shopping for home entertainment systems, computer processing equipment, electronic organs, computer video games, or a digital watch, one of the highest compliments or sales pitches you will hear is "this represents the state of the art." What was called impossible eighty years ago, and which required a room full of tubes, gadgets, and switches forty years ago, fits on the wrist today. As the state of the art keeps improving, electronic designers and builders tell us we have only seen the beginning.

WORSHIP—THE STATE OF THE ART

Art is a demanding taskmaster and on occasion has been known to replace God as the object of worship. The state of the art in construction, electronics, film making, music, painting, and expressions of all manner of human creativity have the technical capability to be at an all time high in our period. However, to the chagrin of many who consider themselves artistically aware, this is a time of great frustration and mediocrity among the Christian community and beyond. The state of the art is in a constant state of change—sometimes to delight, sometimes to dismay—but change it does and change it will!

Our colleges and conservatories are replete with students who pursue the arts and ignore the Master of creativity. The artist has high standards and this is good. Anyone who seriously performs music is in pursuit of the elusive "perfect" performance. No matter how well a great performer renders the piece, it is not quite right; it can always be improved. This is a driving force which cannot be satisfied; ever to be satisfied may mean a decline in excellence, a contentment with mediocrity.

Once, when Gordon was conducting a performance of the masterful "German Requiem" by Johannes Brahms, a member of the cello section gave words to a notion held by many fine musicians. When Gordon spoke with him regarding any personal commitment to the truth he was expressing artistically, he said, "My cello is all the religion I need; beautiful tone is my highest spiritual pleasure and fulfillment." You see, true worship *can* be sacrificed on the altar of the arts. He felt no need to pursue a relationship with God. What could have been a stepping stone to spiritual truth for him was a stumbling block.

Is "Artistic" Unchristian?

Conversely, some Christians seem to believe that to be artistic is somehow unspiritual. They seem intentionally to avoid artistic pursuit and excellence so they will not fall into a possible trap of placing the art above God. We will see as we continue our thinking that true biblical spirituality and true artistic integrity are not mutually exclusive; one is aided by the other when our hearts are bent on bringing to God the honor and glory He requires of us!

There have been artistically gifted Christians who have given up their artistic pursuit because the art was "taking them away from God," or the practice requirements were so great as to forbid time to serve God. While it is not our purpose to judge heart motive, we can but wonder why one could not dedicate his art to the glory of God as an expression of worship. This is a fulfilling of the godly attribute of creativity. Art form *need not* dominate heart condition; it simply must come under the control of the Holy Spirit and support the heart in the praise of God.

A STATE OF HEART

Throughout the history of Christian worship we can observe a constant art-form modification. Early Christian worship began with little form, primarily brought from Jewish worship by early converts. This was followed by refinements and embellishments and ultimately so much form that the original purpose became obscure or missed entirely. In turn, this was followed by purifying reform which tended to start the cycle again. The lesson which seems to require constant rediscovery is the fact that worship is not primarily a state of the art but rather a state of heart.

By state of heart we mean the driving desire behind the worship life of the believer. In both Testaments the Scripture is clear regarding the statement of a heart condition.

These words, which I am commanding you today, shall be on your heart.   (Deuteronomy 6:6)

God is the strength of my heart *and my portion forever.*
(Psalm 73:26)

Watch over your heart *with all diligence, for from it flow the springs of life.*   (Proverbs 4:23)

With the heart *man believes, resulting in righteousness.*
(Romans 10:10)

Let us draw near with a sincere heart *in full assurance of faith.*   (Hebrews 10:22; an excellent biblical definition of worship).

When the heart is set upon God, true worship will not depend upon outward stimulus, it will be in constant progress. Exhortations like "Pray without ceasing," and "Seek the Lord and His strength, seek His face continually," or "All you do in word and deed, do to the glory of God," will take on their intended meaning. This means that all of life becomes a worship service. If Christians were devotedly practicing this lifestyle, a corporate service could not miss being a great blessing, for it would simply be a continuation of a worship service begun days (or weeks or months) before.

Heart worship does not defy art worship, for heart worship will give rise to new levels of art which will have tremendous significance. Orders of service will not generate worship, but they can give corporate expression meaningful direction. Beautiful aesthetic surroundings will not generate God-centered worship, but the worshiping heart can take wings in a beautiful setting. Tremendous musical composition and performance cannot create heart worship, but this can give worship expression unlike any language known to man. Art with the proper attitude can be a great expression; but it must begin with a heart in fellowship with God.

THE "IF ONLY" SYNDROME

When corporate worship becomes ineffective, change seems to be called for. Our attempts to change take many forms which we feel will somehow bring us to more pure worship. We seem almost consciously to avoid the real issue, which is heart intent; we build excuses into our thinking. We may say, "If only the place of worship were more beautiful, comfortable, with (or without) visual symbolism—*then* we could truly worship." We may say, "If there were only more awe, more reverence, more a sense of the mystery of God," or "If only people were more relational, and possessed a real sense of warmth and community." Or "If the musical expression were of a higher caliber with the proper recognition that God desires and demands the best art of which man is capable, both in composition and performance," or "If the music were more contemporary, more 'now' so I could understand it—then I could *really* worship!"

In this brief list, perhaps your favorite art-form in worship was not mentioned, but with some thought you could identify your area of concern, your "if only." The real factor in worship is a heart desire for God; the reason it fails to occur in the pew is because it fails to occur in the daily routine of living.

To Love God Is Our *Highest* Calling

The Scripture consistently reminds us of the absolute necessity to enthrone God in the center of our lives. He alone is to be loved and worshiped; He will not share His glory with art-form (although art-form is useful and necessary in enriching our worship, we dare not enthrone it!). The clear warning and command in Deuteronomy 6:5 and following is a call to love and be loyal to God.

> *"And you shall love Yahweh your God*
> *with all your heart*
> *and with all your soul*
> *and with all your might.*

> *"And these words, which I am commanding you today,*
> *shall be on your heart;*

> *"And you shall teach them diligently to your sons and*
> *shall talk of them*
> *when you sit in your house*
> *and when you walk by the way*
> *and when you lie down*
> *and when you rise up."*   (Deuteronomy 6:5ff)

The New Testament records on three occasions (Matthew 22:37; Mark 12:30; and Luke 10:27) this very same mandate to "love the Lord our God." In our day, with the tremendous influence of humanism and desire to please ourselves, we fall far short of the biblical mandate to love God Himself more than anyone or anything. Sometimes we feel we are doing well when we "canonize" a form of worship, or a certain building, or instrument, or harmony, or melody, or rhythm—we might smugly say, "Now we have the formula; now we're really worshiping," only to awaken one day to realize we have the form of godliness but have long since lost the power thereof. The power of God is identified in heart worship.

Again we return to the main theme of our chapter. Worship is not an art condition, it is a heart condition! All of life, for the believer, is to be an act of worship. Throughout Scripture this is emphasized. The Jewish nation again and again was commanded to remain pure before God in worship and loyalty. Work was to be an act of worship; marriage, interpersonal relationships, community dealings, and, of course, the entire religious-sacrificial system were to be purely observed to God's glory. History reveals that when worship degenerated from heart to art, *great* problems arose. (The same is true today. Any activity, if it cannot be done as an act of worship, is to be avoided.) When Israel's worship life began to deteriorate, so did their society and everything they held dear!

In Isaiah 1 we see the evidence of years of failure in the heart of worship, even though the art-form seems to be moving right along. They were still going through the motions, but the meaning had left long ago. The answer for restoration was not to forget the God-prescribed method or act of worship, since it had become meaningless; the answer was a revival of heart motive which would make the art-form relevant. God had specifically required the very sacrificial system under attack in Isaiah 1. He had required burnt offerings and sacrifices. Now in verses 13-15 He says,

> *"Bring your worthless offerings no longer,*
> *their incense is an abomination to Me.*
> *I cannot endure iniquity and the solemn assembly.*
> *So when you spread your hands in prayer,*
> *I will hide my eyes from you.*
> *Yes even though you multiply prayers,*
> *I will not listen.*
> *Your hands are full of bloodshed."*
>
> (Isaiah 1:13, 15, our translation)

The answer then, as now, was to correct the heart condition, but they, like us, would rather change the art. It is so much less costly than a change of the motive! God is gracious, as seen in His very next words.

> *"Come now, and let us reason together,"*
> *says the LORD, "though your sins are as scarlet,*
> *they will be as white as snow;*

though they are red like crimson,
they will be like wool.
If you consent and obey,
you will eat the best of the land;
but if you refuse and rebel,
you will be devoured by the sword."   (Isaiah 1:18-20)

God prefers from us obedience over sacrifice (1 Samuel 15:22). Going through the forms, no matter how sacred they may seem to be, means nothing if the heart is not in the art! Does this mean we should avoid art to gain more heart? Certainly not! This has been a most erroneous assumption far too long in the Church. While it is true that worship is a state of heart, not of art, it is equally true that heart worship devoid of artistic expression is—to the extent it is deprived—impoverished. Heart worship is enriched by the arts. A clear understanding must be gained that art will not give birth to true worship, but true worship will give birth to artistic expression. Art in every form can help us perceive the nature of God. His truth, His being, His attributes, His plan of redemption, His eternal program can all be visualized and realized through artistic expression to the intellect and emotion.

LOOK TO MENDELSSOHN

How artistically expressive is the eternal truth set forth in Mendelssohn's "Elijah," when the composer, with all the musical skill and expression available to him in the high romantic tradition, handles God's communication with the prophet. In chorus #34, "Behold, God the Lord," he refers to the mighty wind which rent the mountains. The tempestuous accompanimental figure musically blows up the storm. The earthquake is portrayed in musical imitative style; the waves of the quake fairly engulf the listener. Finally the fire and heat are described with quick, staccato musical expression. The heat waves are clearly visible to the sensitive eye and ear.

But God was not in the wind or the quake or the fire. When the composer wishes to express the truth of the "still, small voice of

God," once again the musical expression is the ideal vehicle to envision the contrast. The orchestra and chorus come to a beautiful soft texture which, in contrast to the wind, earthquake, and fire, helps the worshiping heart grasp the truth of the still small voice. How art helps the heart to praise here! It confirms and affirms what can be read and said in a language surpassing words. Take away a sensitive, Spirit-led heart attitude, and all you have left is beautiful artistic expression.

LOOK TO BACH

Consider the biblical teaching about the essence of God. He is *one* God, *three* persons. Throughout the ages this concept has caused no end of confusion and frustration to theologian and layman alike. Much has been written and said about this eternal truth. But by no available means is it more beautifully expressed than in the music of Bach's trio sonatas for organ. Musicians through the years have marveled at the artistic excellence of these works. They have one melody in the right hand, one melody in the left, and yet another in the pedal line—all sounding at once, each retaining its own identity, yet together forming beautiful harmony. The composer intended this to be an expression, a tonal picture, of the eternal mystery of the Godhead.

If one has the heart for God, this artistic expression does him great good in grasping the trinitarian truth. If he has interest only in the art, he may enjoy the music but the point is missed! It seems a most unfortunate fact that those who hold fast to biblical doctrines are often so artistically impoverished that these beautiful expressions of eternal truth are totally missed. Conversely, those who are artistically motivated are either intentionally or unwittingly unaware of the spiritual intent and are swept away by the artistic genius. You see, this great art did not lead Bach to true worship, but true worship gave rise to this tremendous artistic expression. The order is not reversed today.

IT'S A MATTER OF FOCUS

How very easy it is for our attention to be drawn to the art rather than to God; but if the heart is so focused upon loving God, suddenly all the art helps us love Him more fully. Numerous are the stories of Christian artisans who have devoted lifetimes to the pursuit of artistic beauty to the praise of God. When they leave the world scene, they leave behind art which is misunderstood and even ignored by the Christian community, the only people who could really grasp the intent.

Many beautiful places of worship built in another day have become mere reflections of the art of another age. Beautiful cathedrals now simply serve as museums crowded with sightseers and tourists, making money for guides, tourist agencies, and clerics. While it is not possible to know the exact spiritual condition and heart motive of all who worked to build such magnificent structures to the glory of God, many thousands of hours and great amounts of money were given to worship through this artistic expression of architectural, structural, and craftsmanlike efforts.

The story is told of a craftsman who had traveled to America from Europe to dedicate his life to some of the detail work of one of this country's grandest places of worship. One day a sightseer was touring the edifice and observed the workman meticulously laboring near the high ceiling on a symbol which could hardly be seen from the floor. What is more, he seemed to be occupied with a detail on the top, even out of view of the most carefully observant worshiper. The sightseer said, "Why are you being so exact; no one can even see the detail you are creating from this distance?" The busy artist replied, not missing a stroke, "God can!"

Our utilitarian society often misses or even scorns the artist's careful efforts. He sees the art as an end in itself, not as a means of presenting to God an expression of worth and praise. God is a God of beauty and detail. His creation gives ample evidence of His attention to detail. Observe the rose, the insect, the animal kingdom, the stellar system. The more carefully we look, the more perfectly beautiful we see it to be. This beauty is a marvelous vehicle for the believer in worship expression. The Lord of detail has seen to every detail of our redemption as surely as He has in all of creation. God uses art to reflect His beauty and creativity; so ought His redeemed children to worship Him.

The stepping stone of art expressed sensually or emotionally can and should give the heart of the Christian wings for worship. To ignore the arts is to rob oneself of one of the greatest insights into the nature of God and His magnificent dealings with mankind. While it is possible to fall into infatuation with the art and miss the spiritual possibilities, it is equally possible to be artistically deprived, to view the arts as "frill" or possibly merely a way to illustrate a lesson, never to realize this great vehicle for heart worship.

God, grant us hungry hearts for You,
and enough artistic integrity
to see You more truly in spirit and in truth.

Chapter 3

God's Desire in Our Worship

"Such People the Father Seeks"

Perhaps one of the most unexpected aspects in a biblical approach to worship is the fact that *God is actively seeking true worshipers*. Our age, so beset by humanism, tends to define all activities in reference to man and what he does. Even Christians cannot easily escape the moods of the age in which we live. We tend to muddle our thoughts with the thoughts filtering in from all around us. When we come to the issue of worship, we find ourselves prone to describe and define even this response in terms of ourselves.

But worship is about God, not man. The worship of God does do many things for us as individuals and as a community. But true worship should be defined in terms of God first of all. Worship is about God, and worship is what God desires from us.

THE TIGER AND THE LADY

In one of his books, Thomas Howard has described our Lord as "Christ the Tiger."[1] An implication of this description is that the Lord Jesus Christ startles us at times with the unexpectedness of His words and actions: Jesus is no pussy-cat! He is Christ the Tiger!

Among the conversations of our Lord in His earthly ministry,

31

one of the most unexpected and profound was the encounter He had with the much-married Samaritan woman at Jacob's well in Sychar, recorded in John 4:4-42. Tourists in the Holy Land today are sometimes left to their own devices when guides scratch an "X" on the ground and inform them that an event in the gospels took place right where they presently stand. But the well of Jacob in Sychar is not an imaginary, floating location. It is a fixed place which one may visit today. You may even drink water from the well, if you are daring—and you will thirst again if you do so! The place is real and the conversation was stunning.

When the Samaritan woman diverted the conversation from her own troubled domestic life to the theology of worship, she gave our Lord an opportunity to express words that rivet our attention and rock our assumptions. She asked a question about *art;* Jesus responded with the issue of *heart*. She asked Jesus *where* worship ought to be done; Jesus responded with *what* worship is. That is, the woman asked about the state of the art; Jesus responded with an answer that relates to the state of the heart.

These are the central words of this magnificent encounter:

The woman said to Him,
*   "Sir, I perceive that You are a prophet.*
*   Our fathers worshiped in this mountain, and you*
*   people say that in Jerusalem is the place where men*
*   ought to worship."*

Jesus said to her,
*   "Woman, believe Me, an hour is coming when*
*   neither in this mountain, nor in Jerusalem, shall you*
*   worship the Father. You worship that which you do*
*   not know; we worship that which we know, for salva-*
*   tion is from the Jews.*

*   "But an hour is coming, and now is, when the true*
*   worshipers shall worship the Father in spirit and*
*   truth; for such people the Father seeks to be His wor-*
*   shipers.*
*   God is spirit,*

and those who worship Him
must worship in spirit and truth."

(John 4:19-24)

Zane Clark Hodges has summarized the importance of these words, so new and so fresh, in this narrative format.

> Her expectation was not disappointed. She had raised
> the subject of worship, and the Saviour's reply was as
> pregnant a statement on this theme as had ever escaped
> the lips of man. Indeed, once He had uttered it, it would
> be impossible thereafter for any man intelligently to
> ponder this theme without returning to consider those
> priceless words. As an utterance on worship they were
> timeless and absolutely definitive.[2]

Among these timeless and absolutely definitive words are these: *"for such people the Father seeks to be His worshipers"* (v. 23). Many of our questions about worship are like those of the Samaritan woman. We ask where and how questions, for we want to settle issues of form. Jesus' answers cut across form to deal with reality, with spirit and truth.

CAIN AND ABEL

God actively seeks true worshipers. This was not a new truth in the ministry of our Lord. It has always been so. From the earliest recorded acts of worship in human history we are confronted with this fact. Genesis 4 describes the offerings of Cain and Abel. Some readers have assumed that Abel's offering was accepted by God because his offering involved the blood of the firstlings of the flock, whereas the offering of Cain, lacking blood, was unacceptable.[3] It is more likely, however, that Abel's offering was accepted by God because of his heart attitude. Cain's offering of grain or produce was certainly appropriate for a tiller of the ground (see, e.g., Leviticus 2:1, 23:9-14, for later legislation on grain and first fruit offerings).

There must have been an attitudinal difference between the

brothers that caused God to delight in the one and not in the other. The writer of Hebrews explains:

> *By faith Abel offered to God a better sacrifice than Cain, through which he obtained the testimony that he was righteous, God testifying about his gifts, and through faith, though he is dead, he still speaks.*
>
> (Hebrews 11:4)

It was *by his faith* that Abel pleased God. We may assume that Cain lacked the faith of his brother. Further, we may observe that God *"had regard for Abel* and *his offering"* (Genesis 4:4c). It was not the offering alone, but Abel as well that pleased the Lord. Similarly we read, *"but for Cain* and *for his offering He had no regard"* (v. 5a).

Rather than concentrate on why one offering was accepted and another was not, we should really stand amazed that either offering was accepted by God.

The Hebrew verb translated "had regard for" is the word *sha'ah*. This is a word that expresses the concept of "gazing at, looking at, and caring for."[4] From the beginning, God was looking for true worshipers. The Lord Jesus is the One who explains the Father (John 1:18). His explanations are sometimes given in new words, but they are not necessarily new explanations. The Father has desired true worshipers from the beginning of His relationships with mankind.

We should observe that God's desire for worship does not imply that there is something lacking in Himself. He does not *need* our worship. In the eternities that preceded our creation, God has always been complete, perfect, and sufficient. But God the creator desires the adoration of His people. He looks for it. He gazes out for it. He cares about it. When we come like Abel came, we find ourselves in the center of His desire.

THE LAW AND THE PROPHETS

And with the above assertions we find both the Law and the Prophets are in full agreement. One of the splendid texts in the

Torah of Moses that summarizes God's desire for His people is
Deuteronomy 10:12-13.

> *"And now, Israel, what does Yahweh your God require*
> *from you, but to fear Yahweh your God,*
> *to walk in all His ways*
> *and love Him,*
> *and to serve Yahweh your God with all your heart*
> *and with all your soul,*
> *and to keep Yahweh's commandments and His*
> *statutes*
> *which I am commanding you today for your good?"*
> (Deuteronomy 10:12-13)

This text (which builds on the *shema'* of Deuteronomy
6:4-9)[5], uses the Hebrew verb *sha'al*, "to ask," here in the sense
"to require." God has a desire regarding man which He expects,
looks for, and demands.

The emphasis in this text—as in all Scripture—is not on what
the believer does in isolation, but on what the believer *is*, and how
what the believer is relates to what he or she does. Keeping the
commandments is conjoined to loving God; obeying His statutes
proceeds from fearing God; serving God is a matter of one's entire
being. So it is with our worship.

The prophet Micah presented the same point of view some
seven centuries after Moses wrote Deuteronomy. Micah pictures
an individual coming before the Lord asking what is necessary to
be pleasing in His eyes:

> *With what shall I come to Yahweh*
> *And bow myself before the God on high?*
> *Shall I come to Him with burnt offerings,*
> *With yearling calves?*
> *Does Yahweh take delight in thousands of rams,*
> *In ten thousand rivers of oil?*
> *Shall I present my first-born for my rebellious acts,*
> *The fruit of my body for the sin of my soul?*
> (Micah 6:6-7)

In words that begin with clear demands of Scripture (bowing and sacrificing), the claimant then ponders if God is really delighted in the superfluity of animals and oil, or whether even child sacrifice will be demanded to allow one to come before the Lord.

Micah then reminds the questioner of the teaching of Deuteronomy:

> *He has told you, O man, what is good;*
> *And what does Yahweh require of you*
>> *but to do justice,*
>> *to love kindness,*
>> *and to walk humbly with your God?*   (Micah 6:8)

God requires something within us that leads to outward acts of genuine spirituality. The sacrifice of all the cattle of Kansas would avail nothing before the Lord without the inner reality of spirit and truth.

Moses and Micah build on the experience of Abel and lead to the explanation of Jesus: God *desires* true worshipers. He actively seeks those who relate to Him from the inner man, from the heart. True worshipers come before the true God in spirit and truth.

Chapter 3, Notes

[1] Thomas E. Howard, *Christ the Tiger: A Postscript to Dogma* (Philadelphia: Lippincott, 1977).

[2] Zane Clark Hodges, *The Hungry Inherit*, rev. ed. (Portland: Multnomah Press, 1980), p. 18.

[3] The *blood* is not without significance, however. See Hebrews 12:24 (and 9:22).

[4] Hermann J. Austel writes, "The basic idea of *shā'â* is 'to look at with interest.' It is never a casual or disinterested glance." *Theological Workbook of the Old Testament*, ed. R. L. Harris, G. L. Archer, Jr., and B. K. Waltke, 2 vols. (Chicago: Moody Press, 1980), II, p. 944.

[5] Deuteronomy 6:4-9 (along with 11:18-21) serves as the basic *Credo* of Israel. This text is known as the *shema'*, because of the first word of verse 4, which in Hebrew means "Hear!"

Chapter 4

Who Comes to Worship?

"Come, Ye Thankful People, Come"

*T*he success of any book about improving our worship directly
relates to the lives of the worshipers to whom it speaks. The
lack of worship is a symptom; the lack of true worshipers is the root
of the problem.

We suggest that worship is more likely to occur in the community when the individuals of that community realize that *heart
worship* is a style of life. To that end we need to renew our relationship to God and to each other. Our worship will be improved significantly as we develop throughout our congregations three
strengths:

1. A renewed reverence for God,
2. A practice of the presence of God,
3. A deepened sense of the community of God.

Making changes in the structure of the service itself is just
another attempt at dealing with art alone and not with heart. It is we
who need the changes. For then we will come to worship, no matter who is preaching, or singing, or visiting. Far too often, however, we deal with symptoms only.

SYMPTOMS AND CAUSES

A close and dear friend was suffering with a painful foot. Walking was becoming increasingly difficult; access via stairs was excruciating—the foot seemed about to put an end to normal living. Of course, a doctor's help was sought, x-rays were taken, special shoes were worn, bandages were applied, but nothing brought substantial relief. Although causes were sought they could not be found; the best and only thing was to treat symptoms and keep looking for the cause.

One day a mutual friend happened to mention that he had heard of a similar case and suggested the cause to be a bad tooth. Although no toothache had occurred, a dentist was consulted and oral x-rays were taken. Would you believe a small abscess was found which had not yet caused any local pain? A proper procedure by the dentist brought almost immediate relief to the foot and it has not hurt since!

Perhaps the church at large and individual Christians suffer a similar problem. There are many areas which "hurt," many needs that seem to scream from pain. At times the anguish threatens to undo the work of ministry. We try for symptom relief—special workshops, counseling sessions for hurting individuals and groups, missionary conferences, evangelism symposiums, special interest conclaves, etc.; but the pain continues and no real "cure" is found.

Could the root problem of our ministry be the tendency of the evangelical community either consciously or by default to fall short of a fully nourished worship life? How are we fully to love one another as Christ has loved us if we do not practice loving God? How can we possibly love lost mankind except to see them as God sees them? We cannot see from His point of view until we know Him. He loved lost sinners so much that He sent His Son, yet many Christian parents discourage their children from vocational Christian service, especially if it calls them far away. Our full time worship commitment calls upon us to "sing in the congregation" and "proclaim Thy name to My brethren" (Hebrews 2:12). In our worship and conversation we must become accustomed to speaking of our God. Christians must "practice their praise" on one another; then it will be much more natural to tell of the goodness of God in the community, the campus, or on the job.

The cause of our failure in evangelism and edification is probably not our programs or plans, though these must have attention. The cause is our failure to understand that heart worship is a lifestyle, not the result of a cleverly planned and presented corporate hour! (This is certainly not to imply we are against well planned and presented corporate worship.)

What then is worship? It is paying attention to God's revelation (both special, the Bible, and general) and responding to it. "Worship is the highest form of love."[1] Or, in the words of William Temple, the late Archbishop of Canterbury, "To worship is to quicken the conscience by the holiness of God, to feed the mind with the truth of God, to purge the imagination by the beauty of God, to open the heart to the love of God, to devote the will to the purpose of God."[2]

Worship is revelation and response. In our day of strong expository preaching, we have become better at *hearing* than *doing* the Word. Hear the Word—receive! Do the Word—respond! Worship means to respond to God. If we fail to respond, worship has probably not occurred.

Consider the classic worship described in Isaiah 6. Here the prophet receives the revelation, and in every case he responds to it. First is the vision of the awesome holiness and power of God (vv. 1-4), then in his response in view of God's perfection he recognizes his own sinful state (v. 5). With his recognition and confession comes God's action of cleansing and forgiveness (vv. 6-7). The Lord reveals His plan and need for a messenger, and the prophet responds with "Here am I, send me" (v. 8). On hearing God's words describing the negative tone Isaiah's ministry would have, and the lack of repentance that would come (vv. 9-10), Isaiah responded again with the words, "How long?" (v. 11).

The pattern of successful worship has not changed. God still reveals His plan and His will; those sensitive to Him still respond. They are not ones who seek and beg for God's will. They know Him, therefore His will is perfectly clear.

The worship service is a rehearsal for life. It outlines the *dialogue* which goes on constantly between God and believers, giving God's word and suggesting the response he wants to hear—response which includes our adoration, our confession, our thanksgiving, our dedication, and our petition. Worship also offers us an opportunity to give ourselves to God in all of life; in token of this, in the worship service we give him our attention as he speaks to us, we give him our praise and adoration, we give him our offerings of money and also of our service in ministry. Finally, worship is *becoming like God* in our total personhood—body, emotions, mind, and will. The worship service allows us to exercise every part of ourselves, in order that our bodies might be God's temple, that our spirit might be moved by his spirit, that our mind might be the mind of Christ, and that our will might be one with the will of God.

True worship then is really all there is to being a Christian, and the worship service is important because of what it represents as a microcosm.[3]

True worshipers are not forced to treat symptoms, because they are in touch with the prime mover. A knowledge of God coming through a knowledge of His Word leads the true worshiper into "fulness of joy."

Let us now look at three areas that are conditional (causes) and not peripheral (symptoms only).

REVERENCE FOR GOD

It is likely that one of the graces most notably lacking in our culture is the concept of respect, reverence, or awe. Many high school classrooms remain blackboard jungles; young people speak of parents as "the old man" or "the old lady"; police are "the fuzz"—and God is the "good buddy."

One of the unforgettable chapel messages Ron heard in student days was given by Professor Zane Clark Hodges at Dallas

Seminary. He spoke on the threefold name of our Savior, the Lord Jesus Christ. In his explanation, Professor Hodges bemoaned the casual and familiar mores of our student culture, when a new graduate, the ink still wet on his diploma, glad-handed his professor with the greeting, "Hi ya, Zane!" The unexpected—and uninvited—use of the professor's first name would likely be regarded by some as a small matter, given the state of the culture in which we live. But it is no small matter by any standard when we breach values of decorum and respect in our interactions with the living God. Professor Hodges went on to explore the significance of the name, the Lord Jesus Christ, and to urge us to honor that name.

A couple of decades ago there was a popular book on everyday prayers that was marked by immediacy to God and a commendable desire to be on regular speaking terms with the Lord. But the manner of address was at times frivolous, and on occasion seemed even to be blasphemous. There was familiarity, but no awe or respect.

GLORY IN HIS NAME

Who comes to worship God? One who has listened well to the words of the poets and prophets concerning the indescribable glory, majesty, and wonder of our God. Hear these sentiments from the Psalms on respect, reverence, and awe for the holy name of God.

> *Ascribe to Yahweh, O mighty ones,*
> *ascribe to Yahweh glory and strength.*
> *Ascribe to Yahweh the glory due His name;*
> *worship Yahweh in the splendor of holiness.*
> (Psalm 29:1-2, our translation)

> *For Yahweh the Most High is awesome,*
> *the great King over all the earth!*
> (Psalm 47: 2bc, our translation)

> *O Yahweh my God, You are very great;*

You are clothed with splendor and majesty.

(Psalm 104:1, NIV)

In point of fact, the name of God is "holy and awesome" (Psalm 111:9), and ought to be given the glory that this blessed word deserves (Psalm 96:8). The commandment not to use the name of God in vain (Exodus 20:7; Deuteronomy 5:11) has its positive counterpart in countless adjurations to bring glory to His name (see, e.g., Revelation 15:4). Indeed, we join with David in happy assent:

O Yahweh, our Lord,
How majestic is your name
in all the earth!   (Psalm 8:9, our translation)

A GREAT GOD—A TRIVIAL AGE

We have to recognize that we live in a trivializing age where values are askew and attitudes are akimbo. Media-inflated personalities of barely perceptible talent and less taste are adulated; genuine heroes of the Republic are condemned, and the true saints of God are ignored. Attitudes of reverence for God are difficult to find in such an age.

But worship, genuine corporate worship, will only happen when a people gather together in a community response of awe to His name. What we need in our trivializing age is a new and bold perspective on the majesty of God. We agree with Robert W. Bailey that "we cannot worship rightly until we recapture, as the principal element in worship, the overwhelming sense of awe and reverence in the presence of God."[4]

HEAVEN CAME DOWN

The Old and New Testament passages of theophany (an appearance of God) and epiphany (a coming down of God) can be used in a dramatic fashion to reshape and redirect our sometimes shortchanged views of God. Psalm 18 affords a vivid example of the majesty and might of God in epiphany. Verses 7-15 describe in poetic language God's wrathful descent to this earth. The devices the poets use in contexts such as this often include *clouds, thunder,* and *darkness.* In this passage we read of clouds in the lines:

> *He parted the heavens and came down,*
> dark clouds *were under his feet.*   (v. 9, our translation)

Thunder is described:

> *Yahweh* thundered *from heaven;*
> *the voice of the Most High roared.*   (v. 13)

And darkness covers him:

> *He made* darkness *His covering, His canopy around*
> *Him . . . the dark rain clouds of the sky.*   (v. 11)

As we read this Psalm which describes God's wrathful descent, we find ourselves amazed; we shrink back in awe and wonder. We hear figurative words describing realities we can barely comprehend:

> *The earth trembled and quaked,*
>   *and the foundations of the mountains shook;*
>   *they trembled because He was angry.*

> *Smoke rose from His nostrils;*
>   *consuming fire came from His mouth,*
>   *burning coals blazed out of it.*   (vv. 7-8)

It is when we realize that these words of terror and devastation are occasioned as God responds to the *prayer of a believer* that we are truly overcome! It is in response to David's prayer,

> *I cried to my God for help*   (v. 6)

that this epiphany transpired. God's wrath against the enemies constraining David His servant is displayed for the good of His own.

> *He reached down from on high*
>   *and took hold of me;*
> *He drew me out of deep waters.*   (v. 16)

The awesome majesty and terrifying wrath of God described in Psalm 18 in poetic language that stirs the reader to the depths of his or her inner being—this all exists to demonstrate that God will turn the earth upside down, if need be, to meet the needs of His people.

A passage like Psalm 18 admits of no trivializing of God.

A TASTE OF ETERNITY

Many passages of Scripture lead us to just such a conclusion of magnificence and solemnity. One New Testament passage of quite a different sort than Psalm 18 leaves the thoughtful reader with the same level of awe and wonder in response to the greatness of God. This is the gospel account of the transfiguration of our Lord. As recorded by Matthew, this text does not have the rhetorical flourish and poetic flair of Psalm 18. But it is a text that cannot leave the reader unmoved.

The Lord Jesus Christ was on a high mountain with His inner circle, Peter, James, and John.

> *There he was transfigured before them.*
> *His face shone like the sun,*
> *and his clothes became as white as the light.*

> *Just then there appeared before them*
> *Moses and Elijah,*
> *talking with Jesus.*   (Matthew 17:2-3, NIV)

In these few simple words, with one leading verb and two metaphors, we see Jesus the man now Jesus the God. The two principal luminaries of the Old Testament, Moses and Elijah, are at His side in resurrection bodies—a taste of eternity in a touch of time!

Following Peter's feeble words, suggesting a building committee should commemorate the event (!), then there came grand words of the Father from a hovering cloud.

> *While he was still speaking,*
> *a bright cloud enveloped them,*
> *and a voice from the cloud said,*

> *"This is my Son, whom I love;*
> *with him I am well pleased.*
>   *Listen to him!"*   (Matthew 17:5, NIV)

To the prone and terrified disciples comes now Jesus the Man with a gentle touch and a kind word. When they opened their eyes,

> *they saw no one except Jesus.*   (v. 8)

ENOUGH WITH TRIVIALITIES

Who may we expect will come to worship God? It is that woman who has read words describing His majesty and who desires to respond rightly to Him. It is that man who through the liberating words of Scripture has experienced His wonder. It will be boys and girls whose parents refuse to allow them to be molded in the spirit of today's trivializing age, but who rather are helping their children to be transformed by the renewal of their minds to the majesty of God.

Who on reading Psalm 18 can continue to sing "O Lordie" in a chorus like "Do Lord"? Who, on reading Matthew 17, can join in the impoverished chorus to "Give Me Oil in My Lamp," the trivial words about Jesus: "He's the salt on my Frito"? We do not wish to take the enjoyment out of knowing God; but in knowing GOD we no longer wish to be cheap or silly or trivial in our responses to Him. Nothing is trivial in these words:

> *Therefore, since we are receiving a kingdom*
> *that cannot be shaken,*
>   *let us be thankful,*
>   *and so worship God acceptably*
>   *with reverence and awe,*
> *for our God is a consuming fire.*
>   (Hebrews 12:28-29, NIV)

Sometimes people say, "If only I could *see* Jesus . . ." By this, they seem to suggest that all troubles of doubt and discouragement would then be past. But as Moishe Rosen, the leader of the

Jews for Jesus, has suggested, it would be no comfort for one to see Jesus if that person were not prepared for that sight. The experiences of those in the Old and New Testaments considered worthy to see God, however veiled was His glory, were uniformly experiences of a sense of unworthiness before Him.

Our confident hope, of course, is that when we shall see Jesus we shall be prepared for that sight. Because of the Father's lavish love we who are in Christ are now indeed the children of God. We do not know fully what is ahead for us,

> *but we know that when he appears,*
> *we shall be like him,*
> *for we shall see him as he is.*   (1 John 3:2, NIV)

PRACTICE HIS PRESENCE

Who is that person who comes to the community to worship God? It is that man or woman who practices the presence of God in private moments. That is, in addition to holding God in awesome reverence, they *know* Him in daily living. One well-known television advocate of daily exercising instructs his listeners to practice exercises of posture by using familiar objects as memory stimuli. For example, he suggests that whenever one walks through a doorway, he or she might use that structural entrance way to be a reminder to hold in one's tummy and stand up straight.

Perhaps the only physical stimulus most of us have in daily living to cause us to think of God is our food. It is right to adore God in table prayers before our meals, for He is the ultimate source of every blessing (see Psalm 111:5). We should attempt to expand our stimuli to practice the presence of God. A key text that speaks to this issue is the well-known sentiment from the Book of Proverbs.

> *Trust in Yahweh with all your heart,*
> *And do not lean on your own understanding.*
> *In all your ways acknowledge Him,*
> *And He will make your paths straight.*
>
>   (Proverbs 3:5-6)

The verb translated "acknowledge" is a word that speaks of knowing actively the presence of God. One is to *know* God in daily activities. We are to experience His presence in the most mundane of our chores. It is possible to be a minister preaching a sermon in a church without having thought of God in a personal way. It is also quite possible for a woman to be exquisitely blessed by the consciousness of God's presence while she washes some dirty pots. Her husband can know God as he changes the baby's diaper.

All of us have had times of knowing the presence of God in private moments. It takes work to have such experiences on a regular basis. We have been in services of worship where we have been strangely moved by the presence of God; we have also known His presence while driving alone in our cars. We have been at campfire meetings where our only thought was of God; we could as well be walking in a crowd and know Him.

The writings of Anne Ortlund often emphasize the concept of practicing the presence of God. She suggests that one might have conscious stimuli in daily living that may be used to remind ourselves that He is God and that we are His people.[5] As a Jewish family places a *mezuzah* at the door of their home to mark out that house as one devoted to the God of Torah, so a Christian father might use the front door of his home as a memory device to pray for his family and their relationship to the Lord. Every time that father enters or leaves his home, it might be with words of benediction, allowing the door itself to be a prod to pray.

A HOLY PLACE

We may also use *locations* for certain actions. One writer of Western fiction, Louis L'Amour, boasts that he can write anywhere and at any time. Most of us, however, find that we usually do a better job at a given task when we have a specific physical location for that task. A meal at the table is immeasurably more enjoyable than one eaten standing at the stove. When we have a specific location for a task we are also more likely to do that task, For example, Ron does not read light fiction at his study desk, Such might get to be a pattern and serious study might never be accomplished!

One can (and ought to) pray anywhere. But uninterrupted and intensive prayer is more likely to take place in a specific location where prayer is the expected and regular task. At our seminary we have recently established a prayer room. The lighting is soft, there are provisions for kneeling; it is a specific location where praying is done. It is amazing how one's praying can be improved by mutual stimulation and with a specific location to practice the presence of God. It is likely that we will all pray more often during the day in many places, given the specific, regular exercises in a closet.

Make a place, a holy place, for your private moments of enjoying God. Let it be a quiet place, a place away from Muzak and television, from records and radio. Let it be a place where you may be still and know the living God.

COMMUNITY OF GOD

Who comes to worship God? Those who hold Him in reverence and who practice His presence as a way of life. Those also come to worship who feel that they are a part of the *worshiping community*. By stressing individual worship, we might imply that corporate worship is thereby unnecessary. Such is not true.

The fact that some believers do not come to worship God in the community is not a new problem. In the early Church there were already some who believed they could be sufficient before God in and of themselves. To such ones then—and now—come the words:

> *And let us consider one another*
> *so as to stir up love and good works,*
> *not forsaking the assembling of ourselves together*
> *as is the manner of some,*
> *but exhorting one another,*
> *and so much the more*
> *as you see the Day approaching.*
> (Hebrews 10:24, 25, NKJV)

The point is this: We need each other as we worship God. Both Testaments stress the concept of the *people* of God. It is in the *community* that the dynamics of worship are deepened. It is in the flow of people interacting that worship will be broadened.

The Old Testament term *'am* ("people") is a warm word, expressive of mutual dependence, interaction, and cohesiveness. One does not leave the *'am*, the community, for it is in the community that God is basically at work. Elimelech erred grievously when he went to Moab with his family (Ruth 1). By going to a different nation he, in effect, cut himself off from his people and from the blessing of God. We are responsible to God as individuals, but we worship Him best together.

THE FAMILY OF GOD

What a mystery it is to be a part of the people of God! Some of us have relatives who are without the faith. The fact that they are our relatives certainly places a bond between us. Yet one can meet a stranger on a plane, even one from an entirely different ethnic background, and find within just a few words a closeness that surpasses that of family or kinship, when it is discovered that both are a part of the family of God.

Ron was singing one day in southern Luzon Province with a group of Filipino pastors at a pastor's conference. In one of the English hymns we sang there was a line that read "as we travel this sod." A Filipino brother asked what the word "sod" meant. After the explanation, this pastor then said, "That's a new word to me. But I have long known what it meant by the next words, 'the family of God.'"

When we come together to worship God, we do so as a family. We come as brothers and sisters, mutually to stimulate one another.

Hear these words from the Psalms:

How good and pleasant it is
when brothers live together in unity!

(Psalm 133:1, NIV)

The unity of the people of God is compared to precious oil used to refresh a traveler in an ancient day (v. 2), and to the dew of Mount Hermon that brings delight to a distant place (v. 3). It is in fact the blessing of the Lord.

Listen to these words from the New Testament:

Keep on loving each other as brothers.
                          (Hebrews 13:1, NIV)

Be devoted to one another in brotherly love.
Honor one another above yourselves.
                          (Romans 12:10, NIV)

Such words are hardly isolated. They are frequent and compelling. We need to heed them.

How shall we respond to that person who says, "When I come to church I don't come to shake hands; I come to worship God"? An appropriate response would be to comment that people are more likely to worship God *together* when they have first shown their interest in and love for each other.

In our desire to quell the tumult that comes just before many worship services, and which often intrudes upon the services, we may be in danger of cutting the few fragile bonds that we still have in our harried age. Rather than say that people should be quiet as the service begins, would it not be better to provide a place for talking and touching before the service, so that when the service begins there is a community ready for it?

Coffee and doughnuts may not be of the highest nutritional value for one's health and fitness. But these breakfast goodies may be one of the finest means of prompting a sense of community in our churches today. As people sip, their elbows will likely bump others. Talking and touching need to happen for a sense of community to develop. We are in this together; together we need to know it.[6]

A few of the many "community developers" include:
Small group Bible studies
Growth groups
Church dinners

Missionary support groups
Prayer groups
Sunday school classes
Special interest groups
Men's groups
Women's groups
Children's groups
Youth groups

These are not frills. We need to implement every legitimate means available to draw our members into a sense of community, for vital worship of God happens together. Frank E. Gaebelein, headmaster emeritus of the Stony Brook School, writes,

> Yet to worship with God's people in the church is not optional but imperative, and watching TV services is, except perhaps for "shut-ins," no substitute. We worship God not because we feel like it, but because he *is* God and worship is His due and our necessity.[7]

As You Enter

Who will enter to worship? Those who worship God before they have approached the church building. And when they enter the building, they enter deliberately to do in public that which they have already done in private: to adore the living God. Further, they come to worship together!

There is a lovely evangelical church in Sierra Madre, California, where people truly gather to worship God. All of the warm talk and greetings that characterize Christian people who care about one another is done in the narthex. The doors to the worship center are closed, so that the noise of the narthex does not enter it. At each door is an usher who opens the door as people approach, and— when necessary—points to a small but significant sign which reads that one should enter the service quietly and expectantly.

Those who enter the worship center of a local church on a Sunday morning to worship God in the community are those who hold Him in awe. They are also those who practice His presence in daily living and in private moments. So let us live—and so let us come!

Chapter 4, Notes

[1]Bruce Leafblad, *Music, Worship and the Ministry of the Church* (Portland, Or.: Western Seminary Press, 1977), p. 3.

[2]William Temple, *The Hope of a New World*, p. 30, cited by Donald P. Hustad, *Jubilate! Church Music in the Evangelical Tradition* (Carol Stream, Ill.: Hope, 1981), p. 78.

[3]Hustad, *Jubilate!*, p. 78.

[4]Robert W. Bailey, *New Ways in Christian Worship* (Nashville: Broadman, 1981), pp. 35-36.

[5]We recommend with enthusiasm Anne Ortlund's small but potent book, *Up With Worship* (Glendale: Regal Books, Gospel Light Publishers, 1975).

[6]A fine chapter on the value of touch is found in Gene A. Getz, *Building Up One Another* (Wheaton: Victor Books, 1980). This is Chapter 7, "Greet One Another." The reader may also wish to see Paul Brand and Philip Yancey, *Fearfully and Wonderfully Made* (Grand Rapids: Zondervan, 1980), Chapters 14-19, dealing with skin and touch.

[7]Frank E. Gaebelein, "Heeding the Whole Counsel of God," *Christianity Today*, October 2, 1981, p. 29. © 1981, *Christianity Today*. Used by permission.

Part 2

The Program of Worship

Chapter 5

A Mandate of Balance

"Come, All Christians, Be Committed"

A n increasingly accepted concept of ministry, which has substantial biblical support, indicates that there are three primary
aspects in ministry:

    1. *The ministry of worship,* that act of expressing to God
His infinite worth and glory;

    2. *The ministry of love and unity* among the body of
Christ, including education, edification, admonition, caring,
etc.;

    3. *The ministry of outreach,* including missions in all
forms, witnessing to and winning the lost.

UPREACH, INREACH, OUTREACH

These three aspects can be visualized in several ways: (1)
upreach, (2) inreach, and (3) outreach; or (1) God, (2) ourselves, and (3) others; or (1) to worship, (2) to edify, and (3) to
evangelize; or (1) love God, (2) love one another, (3) love the
world for their salvation.

Perhaps no recent hymn writer has said it better than Eva B.
Lloyd in her hymn, "Come, All Christians, Be Committed." (©
1966, Broadman Press. Used by permission.)

Come, all Christians, be committed
  to the service of the Lord.
Make your lives for him more fitted,
  tune your hearts with one accord.
Come into his courts with gladness,
  each his sacred vows renew,
Turn away from sin and sadness,
  be transformed with life anew.

Of your time and talents give ye,
  they are gifts from God above,
To be used by Christians freely
  to proclaim his wondrous love.
Come again to serve the Savior,
  tithes and off'rings with you bring,
In your work, with him find favor,
  and with joy his praises sing.

God's command to love each other
  is required of ev'ry man.
Showing mercy to a brother
  mirrors his redemptive plan.
In compassion he has given
  of his love that is divine;
On the cross sins were forgiven;
  joy and peace are fully thine.

Come in praise and adoration,
  all who on Christ's name believe.
Worship him with consecration,
  grace and love will you receive.
For his grace give him the glory,
  for the Spirit and the Word,
And repeat the gospel story
  till all men his name have heard.

The threefold priority of ministry has been diagrammed in
many ways; this we feel says it best:

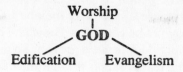

Worship
|
GOD
Edification   Evangelism

Each aspect gives birth and power to each other aspect. When we worship, we edify; when we edify, we evangelize; when we evangelize, we worship. The cycle is endless, but stops when one part is omitted.

All of ministry stems from knowledge of the person of God. To know Him is to love Him. To know Him is to love His people. To know Him is to have godly concern for the lost at home and abroad.

For the sake of our visualization of this model, it is essential to have God exactly in the center. All of the ministry must revolve around Him. If we get the idea that He is interested in our concentrating in only one area, we will fall out of balance! We must keep the lines of the triangle equal in length. Any time in history that the Church has begun to emphasize one aspect of ministry to the neglect of another, to the extent that any has been neglected the Church has suffered.

WORSHIP, BODY-LIFE, OR MISSIONS?

Suppose it is determined by some influential leader that the only ministry of real importance to God is corporate worship. All resources—financial, creative, program, and people—are poured into worship activity. Perhaps new forms and liturgies are developed, new music constantly composed and performed (all objective and praise-centered), fine symbol-laden buildings are built to focus the attention upward, all sermon material is God-centered, and the ordinances are consistently observed with careful vertical attention.

History indicates that this kind of attention may lead to new artistic highs (too often degenerating from heart worship to art form), great sensitivity to the awe and mystery of God, and won-

derful biblical participation by the congregants. The problem is
that attention to the life of the body may be ignored: individuals
deeply hurting may not be cared for. Basic and blessed Bible doctrine may not be taught for healthy growth. So much attention may
be spent on worship that missions may be underfunded and care for
the lost in the very church neighborhood may be missing. Balance
is the keynote!

Sometimes a pastor and people alight upon the notion that we
exist to meet one another's needs. Virtually all programs and resources are focused inward. Love for one another is taught and vi-
sually demonstrated. Body-life flourishes. Superior programs of
training and education are implemented. Activity is geared toward
fellowship with a great sense of family, a feeling that we all belong. We get the idea that God is pleased when He sees His children thoroughly meeting internal needs. It is quite easy and very
rewarding to adopt this ministry concept, but balance may still be
missing.

In every generation there is the call of missions. Untold millions still are untold, the great commission is ever before us, and
the responsibility lies with us in the here and now. It is not difficult
to see how a people can come to the conclusion that outreach is our
most important product. Fund drives, missionary conferences,
mission teams, conferences on evangelism, constant evangelistic
preaching, occasional motivation by guilt—all are the usual fare of
this approach to ministry. There is no question that missions is an
exceedingly important aspect of ministry; but once again we would
sound the refrain—balance is needed!

It Is All There!

The Acts account of the early Church demonstrates the
threefold commitment to ministry. There was a sense of awe, worship, and adoration (2:43); there was a sense of community, be-
longing, unity, and sincerity (2:46); there was an urgent sense of
outreach and the Lord added to the Church daily (2:47).

The Apostle John again rings the truth of threefold ministry
in John 15. In verses 1-11 we are reminded of the joy and responsi-

bility to abide in the vine. This requires one who knows God and strives to know Him more every day. By sensitively abiding in the vine God is glorified (v. 8), and we are fulfilled with sensitivity to Him. In the corporate setting this will involve God-centered activity, objective praise, and an appropriate sense of awe and holiness. In verses 12-17 we have the repeated call and command to *love*. It is not given as an option, it is a command. We are to love and care for one another just as Christ loves and cares for us. Talk about inreach, education, edification! This is a rich and significant responsibility for every believer. A balanced ministry will seek to lead in loving God and one another.

The final third of John 15 (verse 18-27) addresses our responsibility to the world and the lost. We are not to be surprised if the world hates us; it hated our Lord first. We know from this passage and elsewhere that we are to bear witness also that those who do not know our Lord may come to Him in believing faith in order that they, too, may worship Him. It has been well said that the purpose of evangelism is to make worshipers of rebels. That was why Christ came to offer payment for sin and peace with God, bringing the creature and the Creator together in fellowship and worship. In the process the rebel is saved from the penalty of sin (death) and made a joint-heir with Christ with His Christian brothers and sisters.

THE KEY IS BALANCE

We see, then, the validity of the threefold commitment to ministry—the key is balance.

1. *Personal balance*. Individually, Christians may base their entire lives and activities on these questions: What have I done today to worship God in awe and wonder? What have I done today to help a brother in Christ, to comfort, confront, teach, disciple? What have I done today to witness to one outside of the household of faith? It will also influence and regulate our activities. One may ask, can and will this activity glorify God? Will it cause a brother to grow or to stumble? Will it present a clear, posi-

tive witness to unbelievers?

2. *Corporate balance*. When Christians gather together, meetings should be planned to address all aspects of ministry. Certainly individual meetings should have specific direction and emphasis, but each should also include elements with direct attention to God, to the body, and to the unbelieving world.

A meeting called a worship service ought to draw primary attention to the person and praise of God. Well-planned congregational involvement, artistically composed, rehearsed, and presented music should be God-ward. The message spoken should not only be about God, His attributes, His dealing with men, it also should itself *be* an act of worship. The sermon should be prepared and presented not only with artistic rhetoric but theological integrity. The same service could and should be clearly edifying, giving occasion to express love and concern among the body and to present the basics of salvation clearly.

In another meeting, the primary emphasis will be fellowship or meeting body needs. Opportunities for testimony, prayer, and singing of subjective songs of what Christ means to me should be balanced with expressions of worshipful, God-ward activity. Meetings planned for evangelism, using multiple means of attracting and holding the attention of the lost so the gospel can be clearly proclaimed, can and should contain those elements of worship and edification allowing the complete picture to be presented to the seeking soul.

A Life Principle

In any and all areas of life, balance is perhaps one of our greatest challenges. We become interested and motivated in a specific endeavor, and forget other aspects, often to our own and others' harm. One can become so involved in work that he is unable to relax, or so involved in the pursuit of recreation that he fails to produce substance for living. A man may be so involved in his family that he cannot see his ministry, or so involved in ministry that his family disintegrates. Oh God, give us balance!—the ability to invest just the right amounts of the essentials to keep squarely on track!

Individuals, families, and churches must take constant account of investments of time, energy, and resources in the three aspects of ministry. Does our budget reflect equal commitment to worship, edification, and outreach? Do musical instruments and facilities, tools for worship, get their proper attention? Are we investing proper and balanced resources in evangelism and inreach? There are many strategic ways to weigh our resources; ministry demands balance.

Chapter 6

Planning for Worship

"Gladly for Aye We Adore Him"

*T*o worship God in spirit and truth in this age of media-experi-
ence saturation requires a plan. Since the earliest worship experiences mentioned in Scripture and through the recorded history
of the Church, a plan for corporate worship has been in order. The
problem is that a plan is part of the art of worship; but as we have
pointed out, worship is ultimately a state of the heart. Remember,
though, heart worship gives rise to the finest art available in expression. Therefore, a biblical plan is surely indicated!

FREE TO PLAN

There has long been monumental discussion, schism, and
sacrifice over the issue of liturgy, which is basically any definite
plan for public worship. Is it biblical? Is it practical? Does it unify
or divide? Plans for worship have been taken to extremes where
every word and action has been spelled out by a "higher authority"
(i.e., a bishop or council or pope, etc.). There may be, then, no
sense of the immediate, no sense of spontaneity. Or conversely,
planning has been totally ignored and forsaken as unacceptable and
Spirit quenching. From it the entire free church movement has de-
parted. One of the main issues of the title free church is to establish

clearly the fact that we are *not bound* to any earthly authority which, among other things, could dictate how we worship.

One thing must be constantly remembered about the essence of freedom; it not only removes responsibility to another, it brings with it a totally new level of responsibility. It is not merely freedom *from*, it is freedom *to*. It is not unlike the way the freedom from the guilt and penalty of sin is also the freedom to the captivity to Christ. Or, as some in our land would have us believe, freedom of religion is equal to freedom from religion. Real freedom, whether political, biblical, or personal, always brings a higher level of responsibility.

In the issue of planning and preparing our corporate service, then, this means we are free to plan, not free from planning. Much which is very helpful can be gained from a careful understanding of the advantages of established liturgies. Of course, we are not calling for a return to strict liturgical thinking. Rather, we seek to be open to what can be learned which will aid our corporate assembly.

A LOOK AT LITURGY

Gordon was born into a Christian family of the fundamental, Baptist persuasion. He had known only the Baptist way of doing things his entire life, which involved no liturgy and all too little planning. Upon entrance into college, while studying organ, he first heard of the liturgical year because composer J. S. Bach (and others) had written so much music associated with it. While teaching public high school, years later, he had occasion to direct choral performances in some liturgical services on tours. Upon closer examination of the prayerbooks and missals used, it became evident that there was much there of biblical truth and dogma which fit perfectly into Baptist doctrine, just more beautifully and meaningfully organized! With some objective study, one can see several advantages in liturgical awareness while holding (with new appreciation) to the blessings and advantages of the free church.

Conversely, Ron was brought up in a liturgical church with all of the associations of the Church year and the stipulations for the order of service a regular part of his experiences. As is sometimes the case, he found a new freedom and liberty upon attending services in free churches which he had rarely experienced as a youth. Our point is that there are advantages to each system.

The word liturgy is in fact a beautiful word expressive of the work of the people in worship. *Liturgy* has a Greek derivation. It is composed of two elements: *laos* and *ergon,* people and work. The underlying concept of this word is that worship is not a performance that we observe, but a service that we do.

Following are some liturgical advantages.

1. The entire year is planned so special seasons and events in Christian truth are given regular, periodic attention. This includes: (a) Advent (events to and around Christmas), (b) the old and new year, (c) Song of Simeon (I have seen God's salvation), (d) Passion (events surrounding our Lord's suffering and death), (e) Easter (events around His resurrection), (f) Ascension, (g) Pentecost (when did your church last celebrate this most important "Birthday"?), (h) Trinity.

2. Each service within the year has a clearly established goal. The entire period of worship is designed to establish and reinforce this goal.

3. The Scriptures are systematically read; most services include readings from the Old Testament, the Gospels, and the Epistles.

4. The services are planned to give the congregants ample opportunity for participation, both verbal and physical.

5. Various creeds encourage Scripture portions and statements to be memorized and recited in a variety of ways to affirm basic dogma.

6. The music portions of the service are planned to state truth, respond in fellowship, and balance the spoken portions.[1]

Among most free churches special attention is given to the Christmas and Easter seasons, but great and good teaching could be a real part of our corporate lives if some of these other occasions were made more special. It would at least give regular rehearsal to the principal teachings of Scripture as they apply to the community of the redeemed.

Problems with Liturgy

There are some clearly identifiable disadvantages to the liturgical plan which should be mentioned.

1. Being bound to a yearly plan could give too little time and attention to address current needs and subjects.

2. Being bound to a service "theme" could restrict the expositional preaching-teaching ministry necessary for balanced growth.

3. Prescribed Scripture reading may not be directly fitting to the study of that particular day (although public reading of Scripture is called for in 1 Timothy 4:13, and it is *always* profitable and instructive, 2 Timothy 3:16).

4. Congregational participation may become a rote "thing to do." Thoughtless tongues can rehearse much wonderful truth with the heart long out of the picture. Kneeling, standing, bowing, etc., can be done in utter hypocrisy.

5. Memorized creeds and Scripture portions could be just another empty-headed repetition, and God despises the activity of worship which is not heart-motivated.

6. Music, however well balanced and rehearsed, must be a heart expression; style and quality, while very important, are really secondary.

Free Church Observance

Upon recognizing some of the advantages and disadvantages of liturgical thinking, let us look at some factors in the free church context.

1. There is a great danger in freedom of planning corporate worship being interpreted as freedom from planning.

2. With no clearly defined objective for each service, the service tends to be bound from point to point in a most unrelated manner.

3. While in most free churches the whole Bible is held in high regard, all too seldom is it read to any major extent in our services. It is assumed we will save time by reading it in

connection with the sermon.

4. Many free churches suffer from too little congregational participation. Our services largely have degenerated to a spectator activity. We hear lots of great truth, but fail to build in response opportunities.

5. Few opportunities are planned into the service for verbal and physical activity of the congregants.

6. Many worship leaders consider mostly verbal stimuli (with some visual stimuli) to be adequate and appropriate.

7. The most important choir in the church is the congregation. All too often their opportunities to sing are few and their quality of participation is half-hearted, partially because it is so limited.

It occurs to us that one of the most serious problems with much free church worship is our tendency toward an avoidance mentality. We tend to avoid "liturgical-seeming" activity because we do not want to be like the Lutherans or Catholics; then we likewise shun the experience-oriented expressions because we are fearful of being dubbed charismatic. We steer a middle road to nothingness if we pursue this thinking too far! The important thing is to use our freedom as an occasion for good planning. Let us not be afraid to use the best advantages of our brothers and sisters to the liturgical or experience sides—they may really have something we are missing!

PLEASE PLAN!

Gordon had been a music leader in his appointed church for over fourteen years, sitting service after service in a position of observing the congregation from the platform of a beautiful building holding about 1200 faithful church attenders. One day a particular chain of unrelated events somehow fell together to form an hour of worship. It went something like this.

The prelude was skillfully played on a very fine organ, but no one paid much attention. The bulletin title gave no clue as to where the congregation was heading so the organist could not have known what was really appropriate. The verbal part of the service began with the aggressive reading of a Psalm of praise followed by an impromptu, urgent plea for Sunday school teachers given by a well intentioned lay leader who really needed help. He tacked on an immediate appeal for two or three to come now to rescue a class of junior boys running around the parking lot! This was followed by a greeting from a recently returned missionary who was doing a great work, but needed (and took) too long to tell about it, frustrating himself as well as others. We then came to the opening hymn (twenty minutes into the service) which had nothing to do with either the teaching or missions. After the hymn, the Scripture was to be read (it was related to the hymn theme) but it was dropped due to the lateness of the hour. And so it went, a parade of unrelated events which could only confuse the aspiring worshiper.

IDENTIFY THE PROBLEM

The person in the pew may not be able to identify the problem; he is only confused and frustrated. The average congregant simply can't change directions that many times. With logical transitions he will follow some changes but eventually his mind will spin into inattention. He may be there physically, but mentally he left at the fourth interruption.

As I sat there watching this parade and the "lost" look on the faces of many in attendance, I began to feel something must be done to draw a net of attention around these dear people of God, a focus point. When we leave a service after an hour or more of worship, we should be able to identify where we have been and how we will respond to the encounter.

In the following pages, we will pursue ways of handling this knotty problem. It has never been easy and there are no pat answers, but we *must* give attention to a logical, flowing, Spirit-led plan for corporate worship! It has been said of many endeavors, but never has it been more true than of corporate worship, "When we fail to plan, we plan to fail!" "But wait," you may say, "if we plan too much ahead, we won't be led by the Spirit." Two responses:

1. The same Holy Spirit who leads at the appointed hour of worship is surely capable of leading sensitive worship

leaders in their planning sessions. (Worship leaders may be pastors and their staffs, worship/music committees, deacons, etc.)[2]

2. The door should always be open to the Holy Spirit's leading, no plans are set in concrete, no tables of stone are inscribed with the order of things; services can be at once planned and spontaneous.

LOOK AT THE OPTIONS

There are certain "givens" in a service of worship; certain things really need to happen. Other elements of the service may change from time to time. The New Testament "givens" are well stated by Don Hustad in his book *Jubilate*.

The New Christian Synagogue (Service of the Word)
Scripture readings (especially the prophets, and including the letters from Paul). "Till I come, attend to the public reading of Scripture . . ." (1 Timothy 4:13). "And when this letter has been read among you, have it read also in the church of the Laodiceans . . ." (Colossians 4:16).

Homily (exposition). "On the first day of the week, when we were gathered together to break bread, Paul talked with them . . . and he prolonged his speech until midnight" (Acts 20:7).

A Confession of Faith. ". . . take hold of the eternal life to which you were called when you made the good confession in the presence of many witnesses" (1 Timothy 6:12). The earliest form of an actual creed may have been as simple as "Jesus Christ is Lord," similar to the Ethiopian eunuch's confession, "I believe that Jesus Christ is the Son of God" (Acts 8:37, KJV).

Singing (of various types). ". . . psalms and hymns and spiritual songs . . ." (Colossians 3:16).

Prayers. "And they devoted themselves to . . . prayers" (Acts 2:42).

Congregational Amen. ". . . how can any one in the position of an outsider say 'Amen' to your thanksgiving when he does not know what you are saying?" (1 Corinthians 14:16).

Collection (alms). "Now concerning the contribution for the saints . . . On the first day of every week, each of you is to put something aside and store it up, as he may prosper, so that contributions need not be made when I come" (1 Corinthians 16:1, 2).

Physical Action. "I desire then that in every place the men should pray, lifting holy hands . . ." (1 Timothy 2:8).

The Continuing Upper Room (Service of the Table)

Thanksgiving (eucharist). "And he took bread, and when he had given thanks . . ." (Luke 22:19).

Remembrance (*anamnesis,* Greek) "Do this, as often as you drink it, in remembrance of me" (1 Corinthians 11:25).

The Anticipation of Christ's Return. "For as often as you eat this bread and drink the cup, you proclaim the Lord's death until he comes" (1 Corinthians 11:26).

Intercession (following the example of Christ in the Upper Room). "When Jesus had spoken these words, he lifted up his eyes to heaven and said, . . . I am not praying for the world but for those whom thou has given me . . ." (John 17:1a, 9b).

The Kiss of Peace (evidently a Jewish practice, continued by early Christians). "So if you are offering your gift at the altar, and there remember that your brother has something against you, leave your gift there before the altar and go; first be reconciled to your brother . . ." (Matthew 5:23, 24). The phrase "kiss of love" or "holy kiss" is found in Romans 16:16, 1 Corinthians 16:20, 1 Thessalonians 5:26, and 1 Peter 5:14.[3]

WHAT IS THE TARGET?

Knowing those parts which a certain service must contain, set out to place them in a meaningful sequence. There is no one "right way." The service builder(s) must consider his resources as well as his objectives on every given occasion. Usually the best way to begin is to determine where you want to come out. To what response do you wish to lead the people when the hour ends? Some have been known to go for it and come out wherever they happen to arrive, not unlike the man who shot a hole into the side of his barn, drew a circle around it, and declared he had hit his target.

To us the best way to begin is with the sermon topic or outline. Where is the message going, how can the other service components help the pastor (speaker) get where he feels led to go? An obvious burden for a pastor, he must notify his other service participants in advance. But it will be well worth the trouble. The point of the hour will be so clear, even before the message, that all involved in a well orchestrated effort will be a part of the success and the blessing!

The nature (style) and message of all musical input must help build the case. The place in the order where music is presented as well as the selections chosen have a bearing on the final outcome of the event. A song about the joy of gathering, like "Brethren, we have met to worship," would come at the start. A text which is a prayer would probably precede or follow a pastoral prayer. A song of appeal for decision should come when an appeal is made.

We must avoid the old tendency to copy an order of service week after week. Enjoy your freedom to be creative. If a solo always precedes the sermon, for example, it will severely limit the range of usable songs or else on occasion be most inappropriate. If the choir sings a jubilant song of praise, it should be placed at an emotional high point of the service. If it is a quiet prayer song, it may fit another time frame.

In any drama, timing is important! Ask any expert in communication. The right action at the wrong time is worse than no action at all. And make no mistake, a worship service *is* a dramatic event! When the Creator meets the creature, when the Infinite contacts the finite, when Immortal meets mortal, when God reveals and man responds, it is dramatic. If this encounter fails to occur, worship has not taken place even if the bulletin heading reads "Worship Service."

LITURGY IS LOGICAL

Other elements—Scripture reading, responsive litanies, prayers, testimonies, offering-announcements, communion-baptism, sermon (message or homily), and other relevant activities—have a *logical* place to fit in, and that place depends upon the occasion and desired outcome. Look for a moment at the Anglican service of the 1662 prayerbook. Liturgical to be sure, but logical; it is a useful illustration:

(Hymn)
Scripture Sentences (Exhortation)
Confession of Sins and Absolution; Lord's Prayer
Psalms of the Day, each followed by Gloria Patri
    (Glory be to the Father, Son, and Holy Spirit)
Old Testament reading
Canticle Te Deum (a "Glory to God" statement) or a
    Magnificat (My Soul Does Magnify the Lord) Luke
    1:46-55
New Testament reading
Canticle: Benedictus ("Blessed be the Lord God of
            Israel") Luke 1:67-79
        Or Nunc Dimitis ("Lord, now let Thy servant
            depart") Luke 2:28-32
Kyries (calls for mercy); Lord's Prayer or Suffrages;
Collects (Prayers of intercession)
Anthem
Prayer of thanksgiving; Prayer for grace
(Hymn)
Sermon (followed by ascription of praise)
Collection
Hymn

Benediction[4]

While this would seem restrictive to the traditional "free church" thinker, there is an organizational flow which makes a great deal of sense. Notice how the scriptural pattern of revelation and response is followed and emphasized. The service *begins* with Scripture, God speaking directly to the gathering from His inspired Word. It is followed by a time of confession of sin. (The Scripture is clear that the soil needs to be receptive to seeds of truth, and personal and/or corporate sin is a sure quencher to heart worship.) Then comes the Psalm, perhaps praising God for His provision, protection, etc., followed by a brief song of praise about God. Then follows more Scripture, this time from the Old Testament, and another song of response. See the pattern? It is going somewhere. Again, we are not calling for a sell-out to strict liturgy, just an openness to observe some logical progression so that God's people can really sense the nature and experience of worship, of encounter with God.

How to Plan

Here are some questions service planners need to ask themselves about services for which they are responsible.

1. Where is the pastor headed in his message, where does he sense the Spirit of God leading his people? We know of one pastor who is always at least two years ahead in his outlines and sermon titles. He rightly expects his staff to orchestrate all their emphases to be consonant with this direction. He is not *bound* to these sermons, but in many years he has not felt led to change where the Holy Spirit led him to go years before; in fact, he is constantly amazed at how very timely these turn out to be!

2. What "givens" do you feel must be in the service? I.e. hymns, Scriptures, musical expressions, readings, prayers, testimonies, offering, message, greetings, announcements (this list is not intended to be complete).

3. What resources do you have to enable you to realize

these service elements? (Soloists, drama group, excellent readers, choir, someone in whose life God has been doing noteworthy things who could praise and encourage by sharing, stimulating activities and opportunities which need special verbal announcement and support, etc.)

4. What could the service be named or titled which would give all concerned a feeling of direction? It could be a musical title like "Amazing Grace"; then all parts of the service could be titled from short phrases of that great gospel song. Or, it could be the title of the message, or the Scripture used—just look for a title and service order captions which give the thoughts of the participants a train to follow.

5. In what order should these events occur so as to be the most effective? This is somewhat tied to the songs and singers available, as well as to other support help. This is the place where we should really enjoy the freedom of the free church tradition. Some feel, and often rightly, that the sermon should come early in the hour, allowing all else to be a response to it. This could be a good idea, but do not lock it in (don't lock anything in). Perhaps a solo could begin the hour, if the song leads into further activity—possibly it could be sung from an area of the building other than the platform. Some Scripture could be read in a traditional way, but do not overlook the possibility of two or three readers, speaking from various parts of the room. The order of events and the logistics of the service can have a great deal to do with the drama which develops.

BE SENSITIVE!

One word of caution: sensitivity! Be sensitive to the Spirit of God leading. Avoid the temptation to get cute; using creativity just to be different is in very poor taste. God is surely creative, but always in the finest taste. Also, be sensitive to the people God has called you to serve. Lead them into change gently. One of our students once tried to change the spot in the service where the Doxology was sung—he was almost run out of church on the spot. Familiarity is not necessarily a bad thing, but if we are not careful it leads to acting before thinking. Creative, tasteful, appropriately timed change will enhance the worship of even the most deeply entrenched. There are times when we are guilty of trading *ritual*ism for *rutual*ism. Some who consider themselves "non-liturgical" and would defend their freedom at any price have bound themselves to a liturgy even more restrictive than the avowed liturgist. The problem is that all too often the free church liturgy does not make much sense. But there is a definite format or plan followed nevertheless.

We have intentionally avoided the temptation to submit here a suggested order of service. If you like it, you may dig a rut with it and that would defeat the purpose of this whole chapter! We have asked some questions, and answered some. We have tried to show the honest reader the marvelous advantage of being in the free church and the awesome responsibility that freedom brings. The way to plan corporate worship is to begin with the earnest prayer that God will lead, that He will be honored, and that His people will be led in revelation of Him and allowed room to respond to Him. This is so that all will be done decently and in order, and that the divine drama of the God-man encounter would be aided, not frustrated.

In our experiences in ministering in many churches across North America (and to some extent abroad), we have found the same complaint stated by Peter E. Gillquist in his book, *The Physical Side of Being Spiritual*.

> A common complaint I hear over and over again is, "I just don't get anything out of worship."
> Often that statement is accompanied by another: "Our pastor is the best Bible teacher I have ever heard. When that man opens the Scriptures, I really learn. But our church has no sense of worship." There almost appears to be a pattern: the churches that are strongest on the preaching of the Scriptures are often the weakest when it comes to worshiping and giving praise to the Lord.
> People say they feel like bystanders. In most church

worship services there is only one man who gets a workout—the minister. Altogether too many Roman Catholic, Orthodox, Anglican and Protestant churches have been consistently successful in developing congregations of onlookers.[5]

Let's break the pattern of onlooker religion. Worship is meant to be *celebrative*. Worship is designed to be *participative*. Bible teachers will be even better when people come not only to hear, but to do. Let's plan together to worship God in spirit and in truth in our community!

Chapter 6, Notes

[1]An example of a free churchman using the Church year is found in Robert W. Bailey, *New Ways in Christian Worship* (Nashville: Broadman, 1981). See also James F. White, *New Forms of Worship* (Nashville: Abingdon Press, 1971). A reader whose background and experience has been in liturgical churches might smile at the use of the word "new" in these titles!

The reader will profit from reading three writers who are evangelical in theology and liturgical in worship patterns:
Peter E. Gillquist, *The Physical Side of Being Spiritual* (Grand Rapids: Zondervan, 1979), especially pp. 115-126;
Robert E. Webber, *Common Roots: A Call to Evangelical Maturity* (Grand Rapids: Zondervan, 1978), especially pp. 77-114; and
Peter Toon, *Knowing God Through the Liturgy* (Bramcote Notts., Great Britain: Grove Books, 1975), pp. 1-24.

[2]Grady Hardin argues for a worship commission rather than having all aspects planned by the pastor. He says, "Vital worship which involves the people and is a faithful witness and response to the Word cannot be left to one leader or to a merely acceptable order of worship. Churches do not fall into good worship practices." *The Leadership of Worship* (Nashville: Abingdon, 1980), pp. 24-25. Similarly, Wilfred J. Unruh writes, "Strong individual leadership in worship is one way good planning is done, but creativity in a church will often grow when leadership is widely shared. Some leaders find it helpful to involve a *planning team* of perhaps two or three persons." *Planning Congregational Worship* (Scottsdale, Pa.: Mennonite Publishing House, 1978), p. 9.

[3]Donald P. Hustad, *Jubilate! Church Music in the Evangelical Tradition* (Carol Stream, Ill.: Hope, 1981), pp. 92-93. Used by permission. Some of these elements of worship are developed in the latter chapters of our book.

[4]Ibid., p. 112.

[5]Gillquist, *The Physical Side of Being Spiritual*, p. 115.

Chapter 7

The Moods of Worship

"Sometimes Alleluia"

*T*he great need of our day in evangelical churches is for a renewal of worship. We are doing many things well in our
churches. Many improvements are being made in areas of weak-
ness in the past. But our worship still lags far behind our accom-
plishments. Robert Webber of Wheaton College has commented
about evangelicals and worship.

> Worship is the weakest area of evangelical Christianity.
> We are strongest in the areas of evangelism, teaching,
> and fellowship. We are improving greatly in the area of
> servanthood (application of the gospel to social needs)
> and the ministry of healing (counseling and care for the
> emotional needs of people). But depth in the area of
> worship is badly lacking. We hardly know where to
> begin, because we have lost nearly all contact with the
> past.[1]

Where we ought to begin is with the Scriptures. More particularly, where we should begin is in the Book of Psalms. Many
Christians turn to the Book of Psalms in times of stress to find
words of solace and encouragement. Christians also use the Psalms
to give their feelings of great joy the wings of the wind. But it is

surprising, at least to us, how rarely the Psalms are used for instruction. It is as though the Psalms subtly have been deleted from the primary use of Scripture as described by Paul in 1 Timothy 3:16-17. The Psalms, too, are a part of Scripture which God has inspired for our practical use in teaching, reproving, correcting, and training in righteousness, to equip today's believer adequately for the tasks God has for each of us.

One of the great values of the didactic Psalms is that along with the teaching they present, the feeling one is to have about that teaching is presented, too. As people read the Psalms, they may allow the poetry not only to instruct them, but also to give them the experience that great literature may provide. Ron has written along this line in his book on the Psalms, *Praise! A Matter of Life and Breath*.[2]

One of the great teaching Psalms on the subject of worship is Psalm 95. This Psalm presents the moods of worship in a wonderfully balanced manner. God has desires in our worship services today. He has desires not only for *what* is done, but for *how* things are done. In Psalm 95 we find a marvelous blending of a number of moods that God desires us to have as we come before Him in true worship.[3]

Psalm 95 has long been used in the history of the church as a call to worship. In the Latin church, this Psalm is known as "Venite"—"O Come!" This is a Psalm of public exhortation to come, but to come rightly, to worship the living God.

VENITE—WE COME IN JOY

This Psalm, as in the case of many of the shorter hymns of Israel, has three movements to it. In the first strophe (verses 1-5), we have the psalmist exhorting the community to come before the Lord joyfully. Joyfully we come to boast in God our great King. In reading the first words we may find ourselves reading words that seem to be a bit strange. For these words, in a rugged translation, sound like this:

O come, let us give a ringing shout of joy to Yahweh;

> *O come, and let us give a shout of triumph to the Rock*
> *of our salvation!* (v. 1, our translation)[4]

In these words of shouting and boastful adoration we find something about which we might be a little uneasy. We may seem to wish to back up from these words and their implications. Somehow we have decided that in some of our churches the only time to shout is at the business meetings. Yet this Psalm encourages us to shout in adoration of our God.

Now it will not do to say that we are just not a shouting people. For we are, or at least some of us are, a shouting people. It is just that we shout somewhat selectively. Ron has found that he is a shouting person. One summer I took a particularly perverse pride in the fact that I was likely the only one on my country road who canned peaches while listening to the singing of Jussi Bjoerling, the great Swedish tenor. Not many of my country friends know how well peaches go with opera!

My family had picked about five bushels of peaches from a "U-Pick" orchard. The peaches were all ripe at once. Did we have a lot of canning to do! It was about three in the morning. One by one the other family members had dropped off to sleep. I was left with the rest—as was my just dessert. In the orchard a few days before, I kept saying that we should keep on picking, for "we can do them."

Well, the peach juice and the music seemed to go to my head. I was listening to Bjoerling's great recording of the role of Rudalfo in *La Bohème*. At the end of his great first act aria, I felt so moved that I dropped a jar of peaches on the floor as I shouted "bravo!"— and I was doing so to a singer who is no longer living. The music (and the peaches) had affected me so intensely that I was shouting in my kitchen as I was caught up in those lovely sounds. Unless the peach juice was all cleaned up, by the way, I was not likely to be the only one to shout in that kitchen!

You do not have to be an opera fan to shout. You can be a football fan and behave in much the same manner. Ron has a friend who is very reserved and soft-spoken. But from mid-summer until late winter, with a rotary-driven antenna, he receives every football game transmitted in his area. And in the privacy of his living room—for his wife does not enter that room—there are the sounds of the ecstasy of victory and the agony of defeat.

May we say that we have something to be more excited about than a whole choir of Jussi Bjoerlings and than all the athletic teams that have ever been fielded in the person of our God.

This Psalm says, "Venite!" "O come and shout to the Lord." These verbs in the first verse are verbs enjoining encouragement and mutual stimulation. The nature of these verbs may suggest that even people in Israel had to be encouraged to display their enthusiasm for God. They, as we, are instructed to "encourage one another" in public worship—*"and all the more as you see the Day approaching"* (Hebrews 10:25).

The verbs in Psalm 95:1 do not call merely for random sound. Verse 2 channels the enthusiasm of the shout into meaningful praise.

> *Let us come before Him with public acknowledgment;*
> *Let us shout joyfully to Him with melodies.*
>
> (our translation)

We are stimulated by these words to take the enthusiasm that really is a part of our make-up and to channel that energy into constructive words through beautiful melody, thus giving God the honor that is due His name. Further, the words that we use and the music that we play are to be done for Him. It is to Yahweh that we shout in joy. It is to the Risen Christ that we come with words of praise. It is to the Triune God that we make beautiful melodies.

As we think about the application of this mood of worship to our own worship services, we find this mood has a special relevance in the areas of praise and music. This Psalm calls for exuberance and involvement, for joy and excitement as we adore our God and enjoy Him.

A GREAT GOD

The reason for all of the excitement of the first verses of the Psalm is seen in verse 3: There is none like our God.

For Yahweh is a great God,
And a great King above all gods.   (our translation)

As we read the word "great," we may observe that advertising hype and careless usage have teamed together to cheapen the notion of this word. The word great seems hardly enough adjective for this context because of contemporary sloganeering. Other words have assumed more power. One summer, for example, Ron was the other speaker to Dr. Charles Swindoll at Mount Hermon, California, in a family conference. The Allen family went with the Swindoll family for some ice cream on one of the nights. While we were there, Chuck Swindoll in a friendly way turned to our son Craig and asked, "How's the ice cream, Craig?" My boy, who had been affected by a new "in" word at camp, responded: "It's *awesome!*" Now if an ice cream cone is awesome, what word can we use for God?

Yet in Psalm 95:3 the word great is a positive word used in a superlative manner. "God is great" does not suggest that another is greater; there is in fact and in truth none like God. He is great, and He is worthy of our exuberant and excited praise.

Christianity Today ran a splendid article by J. Daniel Baumann on the importance of true worship. Baumann argued in that article that "biblical worship . . . is celebration"—the contention of our message. Baumann explains:

> That is not to say we are to be flippant or careless (see Psalm 89:7), nor that we gather in order to exchange emotional highs and get spiritual goose pimples. When I was a child, I was given to occasional restlessness during church services. I was admonished to "sit still, you're in church." Somehow I got the wrong message. My folks never intended it—but I was getting the impression that God was a grouch; I wasn't convinced I could even enjoy him. I've changed my mind, or, better yet, the Bible is changing my mind.[5]

Baumann then insists that "the characteristic note of Old Testament worship is exhilaration," and he encourages: "Let's have more spiritual celebration; the saints in Scripture did."[6] Such is the mood of Psalm 95.

WHAT OTHER GODS?

In the words of verse 3, "above all gods," we find the admission that in the Old Testament world the issue of polytheism was ever-present. The neighbors of Israel, and at times even some of the people of Israel, believed that there were competing deities. The Psalm says, "No! He is the great One!" His majesty and His regal nature transcend their existence.

That which we have in the next verses is an account of taking out any mythological ideas about our earth. Hear these words:

> *In whose hand are the depths of the earth;*
> *The high peaks of the mountains are His as well.*
> (v. 4, our translation)

The secret and hidden places, and the high and uplifted points—all belong to Him; all are in His control. By using the polarities of deep places and high places, of hidden places and uplifted points—the psalmist rids the world of other gods. For there is no room for other deities if all of the land masses of the earth belong to the Lord. No room, unless perhaps at sea . . .

> *The sea is His, for He made it;*
> *As for the dry ground, His hands formed it.*
> (v. 5, our translation)

There is no room for imaginary gods in the sea either. Both sea and dry ground, both hidden depths and exalted peaks—all are in the control of the One in whom we boast. Emil Fackenheim writes:

For mythological religion the world is "full of gods" (Thales). For biblical man—and hence for both Jew and Christian—the world is radically emptied of the gods because it is the work of God. Mythological man is subject to all sorts of demonic powers. Biblical man worships the God who is wholly beyond nature because he is its Creator. As for nature, biblical man subdues it; for he is bidden to rule the earth which is handed over to him. It is God himself, then, who demythologizes the world, and his act of doing so is the primordial act of grace.[7]

Fackenheim then notes, "In the light of this truth, one must be extremely puzzled by the contemporary talk about the need to demythologize the Bible."[8] What Psalm 95 is saying is that the earth and all that is in it is the Lord's. He has made it and all of the earth is in His control. For that reason, we who know the living Creator God must come before Him with joyful boasting.

The first movement of Psalm 95 thus relates to that mood of worship we may have in our contemporary worship services in the areas of our praise and our music: *Joyfully we come to boast in God our great King*.

VENITE—WE COME IN REVERENCE

The second movement of Psalm 95 has an altogether different mood to it than that we saw in the first five verses. This section still begins with the "venite"—"O come," but now the mood is one of reverence rather than exuberance. In verses 6-7c this is our exhortation: *Reverently we come to adore our Maker and Sustainer*. It is not only with boasting and shouting, with praise and singing; it is also with reverence and adoration that we come before the Lord. Not all of our music is fortissimo; we are not always in the mood for the dance. As Chuck Girard puts it:

"Sometimes alleluia,
Sometimes praise the Lord
Sometimes gently singing
Our hearts in one accord . . . "[9]
© 1974 Dunamis Music. All Rights Reserved. Used by Permission.

It may be that the first words of verse 6 of our Psalm are as

surprising to people in our culture as are the first words of verse 1.
Many of our present worship services are as far removed from the
posture of verse 6 as they are distant from the sound patterns of the
first verse.

The words of verse 6 present images of physical posture as
they represent an inward act of submission. Our physical posture
may be a means of representing our inward submission to the wonder of God's being. So we read in this strophe:

> *O come, let us prostrate ourselves,*
> *let us bow down;*
> *Let us kneel before Yahweh who has made us.*
>
> (v. 6, our translation)

The words of posture of verse 6 call for bowing or kneeling
before the Lord. In Tolkien's masterpiece, *The Hobbit,* there is a
fascinating creature who "likes riddles." His name is Gollum. Are
you like Gollum? Do you like riddles? Here is a riddle: Why is it
that in some high churches people kneel before the Lord, and that
in some low churches people stand with their arms extended to
God, but that in many of our churches we do neither—we merely
sit? Answer that one, "my precious," as Gollum would say to his
listener. You may answer, "Oh, we stand." But do we stand to
adore God, or merely to readjust our frame before the sermon begins?

You may also say, "We kneel." But do we kneel as a community? Or is it not that some kneel in the privacy of their prayer
closets? Ron remembers as a student at Dallas Seminary going on
certain high feast days to the services at First Baptist Church. He
observed that the pastoral staff and the platform party would all
kneel at times of prayer in front of the congregation. But the congregation would stay seated. Why did some kneel and the others
remain in their pews?

We are now delighted to learn that in this great church building there are kneeling units with all of the pews. Presently all the
congregation kneels in prayer before the Lord. The great Bible
teaching of that church is matched by a biblical posture of adoration and submission before the Lord.

The call for kneeling before the Lord that is presented in Psalm 95:6 may seem to some people to be a call for ritual. But our rituals may be a means of expressing genuine feelings of piety. This Psalm calls for an action that describes the reality of obedient adoration of the Almighty God. We are told that once a year, on the Day of Atonement, Jewish people still prostrate themselves before God in orthodox synagogues. We know that on the great Day all men everywhere will finally bow their knees before the Risen Christ (see Philippians 2:10). Why are *we* so hesitant to bow before God now in *our* public services? We shall say more about the posture of worship in another chapter.

His Hand, His Flock

In the first section of our Psalm, the command of verses 1-2 to shout to the Lord was explained in verses 3-5. We are to be exuberant before the Lord because He is our great King. In this second strophe of the Psalm the command to kneel before the Lord (v. 6) is explained in verse 7. We come before Him with reverent adoration because of the relationship we have with Him by His grace.

> *For He is our God*
> *and we are the people of His pasture,*
> *even the flock of His hand.*
>
> (v. 7a-b, our translation)

These words depict the exquisite relationship we have with the God of glory by His grace. Those who have come to the Father through the person of His Son are now a part of His family. The psalmist uses words in unexpected combinations in this verse to describe this relationship. He might have said: *"We are the people of His hand, the flock of His pasture."* But by the more unusual wording, as printed above, the poet heightens our senses to the wonder of it all.

Imagine what it really is to be a part of the people of God! Think on it.

We are the people of His pasture!

We are the very flock of His hand!

How can we not respond in reverent adoration, bowing heads, bending knees, prostrating our beings before God?

Reverently we come before Him. In our reverent adoration we display our acknowledgement that He is our Maker and that it is He who sustains our living. He is the maker of all; He has made us. He is the King of the universe; He holds us in His hand as a shepherd might cuddle a lamb. As we read these words we find our joy is balanced by our adoration. This is another mood of worship. This mood relates to our times of prayer as well as to music of contrition and submission. We come to celebrate with joy; we also come to celebrate God with reverence.

VENITE—WE COME IN FAITH

Now we come to the third movement of Psalm 95. This begins, strangely enough, with the last words of verse 7:

Today, if you will obey His voice . . .

The reader of the New Testament is reminded of the use made of the section by the writer to the Hebrews in chapters 3 and 4 of that great book. But as we look at these words in the context of this Psalm, these words may suggest yet a third mood of worship: *Faithfully we come to obey God our Master*. Thus, the first part of the Psalm with its emphasis upon joyful abandon may relate to our present times of singing and praise; the second part of the Psalm with its emphasis upon reverent adoration may relate to our present times of prayer and reflection; and this third part of the Psalm with its emphasis on faithful obedience may relate to our present times of hearing the preached word.

The words of the last line of verse 7 speak of obeying the voice of God, and they are followed by words of condemnation and exhortation. Is not this suggestive of a sermon that compels the feeling that God is speaking and that God is to be obeyed? The third part of our Psalm seems to relate to the preaching that we ought to be doing, and it relates to the preached word that we ought to be obeying. For today we have an opportunity to obey His voice.

A COVENANT OF ANGER

If you look closely at the words of verses 9-11 in your Bible you will see that these are words with quotation marks about them (see, for example, in the New American Standard Bible). The speaker has changed. God has, as it were, burst into the Psalm. Verses 8-11 are the words of God in admonition, based on the experience of the nation Israel in the past. Here is a terrible condemnation by God of the wilderness community which in rebellion did not obey the words of their Lord.

There were times when the wilderness community did come before God with great joy. There were times when that community came before Him with reverent adoration. But there were also times—terrible times—when that community failed in that third step, when they did not obey His word. This leads to a somber mood for the close of the Psalm. Here there is a call for obedience to the preached word.

We are commanded as a worshiping community today not to allow our hearts to be hardened, as was done by the wilderness community. For when that people hardened their heart, they found themselves cut off from the great blessing that God had desired to give to them:

> *"Do not harden your hearts, as at Meribah*
> *As in the day of Massah in the wilderness;*
> *When your fathers put Me to the test,*
> *They tried Me, even though they had seen My work.*
> *For forty years I loathed that generation,*
> *And said they are a people who err in their heart,*
> *And they do not know My ways.*
> *Therefore I swore in My anger,*
> *Truly they shall not enter into My rest!"*
>
> (vv. 8-11, our translation)

We read of two place names in verse 9, Meribah and Massah. These are used together of two separate occasions in which Israel tested the Lord. These were occasions in which they challenged His right to rule them. They contended with Him; the Hebrew word leads to the place name *Meribah*. They put Him to the test; the Hebrew word leads to the place name *Massah*. Meribah is the place of contention. Massah is the place of testing.

In Exodus 17 we read of the account of Israel in great need of water. In their thirst they challenged God and they condemned His ways. They did not obey God nor believe in Him. God brought water from the rock through the agency of Moses. But this was an occasion for judgment as well.

In Numbers 20 we read much the same story. It is the same song, second stanza. In this occasion even Moses is caught in unbelief and in disobedience; even he experiences God's judgment. For forty years God declares that He was "disgusted" with that generation. Verse 11 of Psalm 95 describes a *covenant of anger* that contrasts sharply with the *covenants of blessing* that animate the Old Testament record. God's anger rested upon that people because they went their own way and did not follow the ways of their God.

The experience of the wilderness community in Exodus 17 and in Numbers 20 serve as a solemn frame to the central picture of rebellion in Numbers 14. There the people of God rejected His word, they rebelled against His promise, and they refused to follow His bidding. An entire generation was condemned to wander in the desert sands, away from the resting place that God had desired to provide for them.

The words of verse 9 are especially touching:

> *When your fathers put Me to the test,*
> *they tried Me,*
> *Even though they had seen My work.*

In our own lives—today—we have an opportunity to hear the word of God proclaimed in the preaching ministry of community worship. In our own lives—today—we tend to err just as Israel did by rejecting His word, rebelling against His promise, and refusing to follow His bidding. And we, like they—today—stand the awful risk of not enjoying in this life the blessings He has awaiting us.

And we, like they, tend to reject and rebel and refuse even though we, too, have seen His work!

It is not enough merely to shout words of praise. It is not enough merely to kneel in adoration. These moods of worship need to be conjoined to faithful obedience to His word. Today we have the opportunity to hear—and do—His word.

In the context of this Psalm, these words of the third movement (vv. 7d-11) are a call for obedience to the word of God as it is proclaimed in our worship services.

VENITE—AND SO LET US COME!

We come together to celebrate.
>   We do so joyfully.
>   We do so reverently.
>   We do so faithfully.

When we do these things, then we will be that kind of people that our Lord Jesus spoke of in John 4:23, true worshipers whom the Father seeks. Then we shall be among that company that worships the living God in spirit and in truth (John 4:24).

Chapter 7, Notes

[1]"Foreword" to Ronald Barclay Allen *Praise! A Matter of Life and Breath* (Nashville: Thomas Nelson, 1980), p. 9.

[2]Ibid., see Chapter 4, "Poetry—The Language of the Psalms," pp. 41-56.

[3]This chapter is an adaptation of a brochure written by Ronald Barclay Allen, *Let Us Celebrate: A Call to Worship* (Portland, Or.: Western Seminary Press, 1981), and is used by permission.

[4]The translation of Psalm 95 in this chapter is a personal translation.

[5]J. Daniel Baumann, "Worship: The Missing Jewel," *Christianity Today* (Nov. 21, 1980), p. 29.

[6]Ibid.

[7]Emil L. Fackenheim, "Man and His World in the Perspective of Judaism: Reflections on Expo '67." *Judaism* 16:2 (Spring, 1967), 170.

[8]Ibid.

[9]Excerpt from "Sometimes Alleluia" by Chuck Girard. Published by Dunamis Music, 8319 Lankershim Blvd., No. Hollywood, California 91605. Used by permission. All rights reserved.

Chapter 8

The Call to Quality

"Give of Your Best to the Master"

*T*he scene is a local church, Anywhere, U.S.A. Once again, almost unexpectedly, it is Sunday. And the worship service is about to begin. A few days ago, Diane was asked to sing for the service because of her nice singing voice. Time slipped by, however, and she failed to find time to prepare. With all the activities of a busy young wife and mother, she had intended to practice, but . . . Since the pastor is counting on it, she would do something. She quickly thumbs through the same book in which she found nothing new the last time, to find a time-worn favorite. Half embarrassed, she hurries to the platform, looks to the anxious pianist, and says, "I hope you know this one!"

Perhaps this week has been unusually difficult:

—Many hospital and pastoral care calls had to be made
—A crisis on the building committee
—A son who played a school game which HAD to be attended
—A marriage crisis in the church family demanded immediate attention
—Without warning, the car broke down, presenting not only transportation trials but dollar doldrums

Almost any local pastor has weeks like this—practically

every week! How can a minister with this schedule possibly prepare and rehearse a message which will not only expound the unsearchable riches of eternal truth, but also have homiletic integrity? How can he present a message which not only teaches truth but is aesthetically attractive? The message should please and edify the congregation, but far more it should praise and glorify God. Not only the message, but the entire service is under the typical pastor's direction. Has he thought and prayed over the general flow of events? Will it be a unified hour in which the people clearly grasp the central focus and emphasis? Or, will it degenerate into a series of unrelated events (like a variety show) where congregants will have little notion of where they have been or what has occurred at the end of the hour? The artistic, well balanced, Spirit-led corporate hour does not fall packaged from the sky; it requires planning and rehearsal.

MERELY GOOD ENOUGH?

Ever wonder why the Church so often stumbles along with worn out or inadequate facilities? As musicians, we are particularly aware of the quality and condition of church instruments. Recently all instruments have become more valuable, but churches seem to have the corner on the community's largest collection of junk pianos. After a piano has seen better days, had a few keys broken, been left in the garage for a few years, been sideswiped by the car, sustained a cracked soundboard and several broken strings, it is given to the church to be used in the service of the King of kings! As children's classes and choirs attempt to sing to these wrecks, young ears and eyes soon get the idea that while we would not have things like these in our home, they are good enough for God.

Musical instruments are not the only example of good enough mentality. Our recent heritage as evangelicals would indicate our compromise and carelessness in the service of Almighty God. We must remember that God is not the author of mediocrity. He demands our best. If, before God, that which some may consider to be junk IS our best, surely He understands and is appropriately responsive to our worship and praise. It must be noted that much empty noise, much "clanging cymbal" (1 Corinthians 13:1) praise has been raised on grand, costly instruments in glorious buildings; but this does not mean that acceptable praise *must* be rendered on junky instruments in terrible, unkept, disgraceful surroundings.

What does God have to say about excellence? What are His requirements of sacrifice? We are to bring to God the "sacrifice of praise" (Hebrews 13:15). We are to present ourselves unto God, a living sacrifice as a "spiritual service of worship" (Romans 12:1, NIV). Excellence must be at the heart of worship and reveal itself in the art of worship expression. 1 Peter 2:9-10 sheds some important light.

> *But you are a chosen people,*
> *a royal priesthood,*
> *a holy nation,*
> *a people belonging to God,*
> > *that you may declare the praises of him*
> > *who called you out of darkness*
> > *into his wonderful light.*
>
> *Once you were not a people,*
> *but now you are the people of God;*
> > *once you had not received mercy,*
> > *but now you have received mercy.*   (NIV)

We are a royal priesthood called to praise. The sacrifice demands our careful attention, our best effort—not thrown-together musical renditions and sermons in poorly-built, run-down facilities on instruments which should have been retired years ago!

At the judgment seat of Christ the works of believers will be judged as to whether they are good or bad. One of the standards for judgment will be excellence in quality. In 1 Corinthians 3:13 we read, *"The fire will test the quality of each man's work."* Since worship is a work of the believer, this too will be judged for its quality.

Our works will also be judged on the basis of our faithfulness

(1 Corinthians 4:2) and motivation (1 Corinthians 4:5).

Since much of our worship is praise to God, it is scarcely to be believed that we may then receive praise from God! (1 Corinthians 4:5) But ultimately the symbols of God's praises to His people, the crowns, will be cast at the feet of King Jesus (as we read in Revelation 4:10, 11).

DAVID AND THE JEBUSITE

In the Old Testament account of King David and Araunah the Jebusite (also called Ornan), recorded in 2 Samuel 24 and 1 Chronicles 21, there is a significant principle of sacrifice. David had sinned against God in numbering his people against the advice and counsel of Joab. The penalty for the sin was terrible; God was already carrying out the sentence, and David knew the only path to his restoration was the path of sacrifice.

The incident came to a climax on the site of the threshing floor of one of David's subjects, Araunah. The king had need of the elements of Old Testament sacrifice: oxen, fuel, and wheat for the grain offering. The faithful subject offered to give these things to the king, for his leader was in desperate need and the solution needed to come quickly. This was no cheap offer; a threshing floor was a priceless piece of real estate, an Israelite's primary possession. The fuel offered was his threshing sledges, not some scrap wood. These represented his ability to feed his family and meet his most basic needs.

But the king, knowing the nature of sacrifice, was not about to present something which was cheap. David insisted upon paying his subject a fair and full price for the materials of sacrifice. A principle for our sacrifice of praise jumps off the biblical account in 1 Chronicles 21:24.

> *But King David said to Ornan (Araunah),*
> *"No, but I will surely buy it for the full price;*
> *for I will not take what is yours for Yahweh,*
> *or offer a burnt offering which costs me nothing."*

THE BEST IS ASSUMED

The biblical definitions and assumptions with regard to sacrifice are well established and consistent. Sacrifices always are to represent the best available to the faithful worshiper, not some poor specimen given with the condescending attitude which says, "God will understand." He doesn't understand in this case; He demands excellence! In the law we observe a complex and beautiful sacrificial system meticulously spelled out by God for the proper maintenance of fellowship with His people. One thing which stands out is that the offerings—whether bulls, goats, lambs, or doves—were to be the *best*, the *finest* in the flock of the faithful (Leviticus 1:10).

In fact, indications of lack of obedience and faithfulness were those occasions when less than the best was offered (Malachi 1:8). Sometimes God's people would (and will) try to find a short cut, something not so costly—and God was most displeased. The temptation is to appear to do what honors God, but without the integrity of intent which demands our best! Satan is most pleased with this kind of hypocrisy. The prince of darkness trembles when God is truly glorified and honored. We, as well as God, know when we are presenting a sacrifice of praise and life which has indeed cost something: our possessions, talent, and time given over to Him to magnify His name and reputation. Cost takes different forms in various disciplines, but here are some examples.

THE BEST IS GOOD ENOUGH!

Sermon preparation. Not every person called to be God's spokesman in the assembly of believers is equally blessed. Some have winsome personalities and a wonderful way with words, a pleasing and persuading public delivery. Some may be excellent students of God's Word, with good command of the literature, complete with an excellent grasp of the biblical languages. Others may be quite plain folk, not exemplary in their presentation, not able to attend fine schools and be well taught.

God has not gifted us equally, nor has He provided for all the availability of fine training. He has given us the same Holy Spirit, the same Spirit of truth, the same power of God. The question is, with what integrity and ambition will we put our abilities and tools to work? The talented, sharp-appearing, quick-minded spokesman with a gift of gab can sometimes do better with little or no careful preparation than the plain person who may study and prepare endlessly. The point is, God expects no more than, no less than, no other than, our very best, our all. He does not hold one accountable for another's abilities and opportunities. To paraphrase Goethe: "In preaching, the best is good enough." [1]

Physical equipment and capital properties. The same can be said for this area of any given local church. Some local churches seem to have no end of buildings, equipment, educational materials, staff positions, and more. Some have almost nothing with which to work: a run-down building in a less than desirable part of the city with virtually no resources to improve anything. It is true that great, God-glorifying work and ministry can be going on in both places. God can work with much and be greatly glorified as His people provide much with the heart fixed on honoring the Lord and Him only. If the old, run-down facility is supported by God's people there, and they are giving their best—it just isn't enough to be impressed by outside observation—it can be a most sweet sacrifice of praise to God. God is neither impressed by opulence nor depressed by poverty. He looks at the heart of His people and knows *exactly* what is going on. It is not the art of the building; it is the heart of the people which pleases God. But remember, heart worship presents the best—that which costs. Therefore the art (surroundings and content) will likely improve.

Musical Expression. All musical talent is from God. No one simply deserves to play or sing very well; the basic tools are inborn. Music and athletics have much in common: coordination, rhythm, discipline, performance pressures, coaching, and skill refinement. The ability of a coach or teacher is inconsequential if the innate ability to perform is absent in the student. A great teacher using all the latest and finest techniques of his craft cannot make the ungifted good. If we are moderately gifted, our musical service will probably be little more than moderately good; our best is all

God expects. If we are extremely gifted, we could well "get by" with little practice and do more, probably better, than most anyone else. But it would fall short of our best.

WE ALL HAVE TALENTS

The well-known parable of the talents speaks volumes to this issue. In Matthew 25 our Lord speaks to the importance of disciplined talent investment. Remember? A man about to go on a journey entrusted to his slaves some talents. One received five, one two, and another one. The one who received five and the one who received two both invested their treasures and were able to return twice the investment. The slave with one (maybe because he was upset for not getting more) hid his talent and made no gain. When the master returned he was upset and took it from him and gave it to the faithful servant who knew what to do with a talent when he had it. The faithful slaves were rewarded because they had realized their potential. Even though they were not equally blessed, they were both productive.

None of us is equally blessed and gifted, but the Lord rightly expects the proportionate return from each investment. In musical service, too many five and two-talent people are doing one talent work because of laziness or the sin of failure to make the God-expected maximum effort. This leaves many one (or less) talent people to do the work of the ministry because of lethargy and spiritual insensitivity. Some complain, "If I were only as good as _____, *then* I would serve." Remember, the biblical principle of sacrifice recognized that all will not be able to bring equal sacrifices, but *all* must bring their best! May we have the artistic, spiritual, and ministerial integrity to bring our sacrifice of praise as believer priests doing our very best, not to the praise of men, but to the glory of God.

To be good in the area of service to which we are called costs something. We are not to offer to God that which costs nothing. Why do we give Him our junk pianos, old clothes, shabby buildings, poorly prepared music, half-ready sermons, last-minute Sunday school lessons—is it any wonder our ministries are not doing well?

Seek help, the best training you can secure. Prepare well, recognize the awesome standards of our sovereign, Creator Lord. Engage in assiduous practice, not to the gratification of the arts, but to the glory of God. It is appropriate for God's people to sacrifice to provide attractive, well-kept facilities for worship and service. Instruments should be maintained in good stewardship, and as a worthy, expressive tool. How can that which is excellent be rendered on out-of-tune, frail instruments? Excellence and beauty and godly attributes; let us reflect Him!

Chapter 8, Notes

[1]Goethe's famous quotation concerns art. Since preaching is (or ought to be) a form of art, we believe the application here to be justified.

For Further Reading

D. Martyn Lloyd-Jones, *Preaching and Preachers*, Zondervan Publishing House, 1971.

Haddon W. Robinson, *Biblical Preaching*, Baker Book House, 1980.

H. R. Rookmaaker, *Art Needs No Justification*, Inter-Varsity Press, 1978.

Franky Schaeffer, *Addicted to Mediocrity*, Crossway Books, 1981.

James S. Stewart, *Heralds of God*, Baker Book House.

Chapter 9

Beauty in Worship

"For the Beauty of the Earth"

G ordon's father was driving his family west in the late 1940s from their home then located in Michigan. Father was a singleminded man with his head set on his destination, minus sidetrips. After much family pressure the decision was made to visit the Grand Canyon, which was considerably off the main thoroughfare. At long last we arrived at the rim of this grand natural phenomenon, and what a sight! The multiple colors and textures, the immensity, the mighty Colorado River seemed dwarfed as it wandered through the bottom. After numerous "oohs" and "ahs" by family members, Dad was still unimpressed.

You see, he had been raised on a West Virginia farm in a rather primitive setting and had worked hours as a boy behind a horse-drawn plow to try to eke out a living from rock-filled ground. After looking at the majestic canyon, all he could observe was "What a wasteland; you couldn't grow any corn there!" He looked at it from a farmer's point of view, and to him what was beautiful was that which was productive. (Between this incident and his homegoing in 1971, he learned a lot about beauty and how to appreciate it. He came to understand that beauty has its own kind of function, and that God's glory can be portrayed in creative expression.)

Sometimes our utilitarian, pragmatic thinking keeps us from a development of aesthetic appreciation. If it works, it is good; if it is just for visual beauty, it is not. Persons with indiscriminating ears sometimes find it difficult to appreciate aural quality. They feel if an instrument "works," that is all it takes. If, when a key is pressed, sound comes out, it is good; little attention is given to the quality of sound. Jazz musicians sometimes kid with each other as they tune up by saying, "Well, that's close enough for jazz!" (Great jazz artists, of course, are uncompromising on quality.) The same mindset concludes that if a building does not leak, and has some heat and light, it is fine. Little or no appreciation is given for its shape or finish texture. It is good and right to give attention to beauty; appreciation of beauty is a step of maturity—especially beauty God has given to draw attention to Himself!

THE LAVISH BEAUTY OF GOD

God surely has room in His creation for beauty; He can afford it. Inherent within His beautiful creation is unsurpassed utility. The thousands of acres in the world's terrain which seem to serve no pragmatic purpose—of which the Grand Canyon is an example—give ample evidence of this fact. Naturalists tell us these seemingly unproductive areas are vital in the whole balance of nature. And how very refreshing and beautiful they are to those who will take time to appreciate them.

Think of the wildflower, beautiful in every detail, perhaps in a remote area seldom seen by man. There it is tossing its beauty in the breeze, showing forth the glory of God. Most of us place value on flowers in our yards; they, too, are so beautiful, so delicate. And they, too, proclaim their Maker's praise!

God sanctioned some fantastic beauty, even opulence, in the building of the temple by David's son, Solomon. Imagine a modern committee's reaction at the suggestion of a full width porch overlaid with pure gold, or of adorning the house with precious stones and using nails of pure gold to hold it together (see 2 Chronicles 3). The beauty of the temple may be regarded as an example of the characteristic spiritual and aesthetic beauty of the believer. Christian, you are the temple of God; He has chosen to indwell you, and beauty must characterize His dwelling place.

> *Do you not know that you are a temple of God,*
> *and that the Spirit of God dwells in you?*
> *If any man destroys the temple of God,*
> *God will destroy him,*
> *for the temple of God is holy,*
> *and that is what you are.*   (1 Corinthians 3:16-17)

GOD-MOTIVATED BEAUTY

Certainly a cultivation of inner beauty comes by spiritual hunger for God-motivated beauty. In Philippians 4:8 we are given good advice.

> *Finally, brethren, whatever is true,*
> *whatever is honorable,*
> *whatever is right,*
> *whatever is pure,*
> *whatever is lovely,*
> *whatever is of good repute,*
> *if there is any excellence*
>   *and if anything worthy of praise,*
> *let your mind dwell on these things.*

As Christians become mature there is likely to be more and more hunger for and production of that which is truly beautiful. We are thinking, not of beauty (or art) for its own sake, but of beauty which draws attention to the Lord of beauty. This beauty is seen in our church buildings (which *are* symbols, either to honor or dishonor), in our symbolism (always conspicuous, even when absent), in our musical expressions (quality of composition and presentation). Beauty ought to be true, honorable, right, pure, lovely, reputable, and praiseworthy. Let beauty declare our Lord's glory, both in public worship and in private adoration of His works.

BEAUTY AND TRUTH—PUBLIC WORSHIP

A theology of beauty in worship should be able to stand tests that relate experience and truth. That is, experiences that we have in our worship services ought to be true experiences and we ought to work for elements in our worship services that will present experiences that are beautiful in truth.

Peter Toon has proposed three tests that one may use to evaluate experiences with God in public worship as well as in private moments. These tests are safeguards against asserted experiences that are misguided, and they are a means of validating genuine experiences with the living God—experiences which are in accordance with beauty and truth. Here are his tests.

1. Is the experience of God's nearness (or power, or love) true to his word? If it becomes tied to a particular building, or a particular minister, or particular music, then it is of equivocal value, and may well fail this test. If at the heart of the "knowledge" there is the God of the Scriptures, and the Jesus whom the New Testament reveals as Savior, all is indeed well.

2. Is the experience of God such as to foster the oneness of the Church of Christ, or such as to damage it? This is a specific application of principle 1, but a sufficiently important one to warrant listing separately. The body of Christ is at worship as one and the experience of God which comes in the sharing together is for the benefit of all, not for private enjoyment. Or, put in another way, any private "encounter" with God of an individual should not lessen his involvement in the worshipping body, even if the experience was in fact private to him, and the opportunity to share the benefit was lacking.

3. Does the experience of God lead to an ethical strengthening, or does it promote holiness? The instances of knowing God [given by some people] might in most cases have no moral implications at all. They might be aesthetic experiences confounded with a knowledge of God. Or they might be slightly masochistically induced flirting with the dangers of coming too close to a holy God, in which the

danger of being caught by God has the air of a delicious thrill, but there is no actual meeting with God.[1]

BEAUTY AND HIS WORKS

Consider the beauty of the starry host. There are so many stars out there that, even with all our advanced technology, we can only estimate the numbers. We have learned much more recently from the tremendous pictures beaming back from our space probes data which confirm and change theories with regard to the details of the galaxies. Regardless of the details, we know for sure that these hosts consume and radiate vast amounts of energy. We have some idea of the energy of our local star, the sun. We know that if it were to fail, all of life as we know it would rapidly fade and freeze. We also know that it is a comparatively small star among the millions God has spread profusely through the heavens. Knowing the tremendous amounts of energy consumed by our sun and multiplying it by even the smallest estimates of stars, we barely begin to grasp the vast amounts of cosmic energy generated.

As far as we know, in the vastness of the universe, apart from our sun, no real utility is served by this energy output. It causes us no emergency when a star burns out; there are lots more to enjoy. Besides, it takes so long for a given star's light to reach us that it might have been burned out for millennia and we would not even know it! Yet, in the Scripture we are told the primary purpose for all this grandeur, this astronomical light show!

The heavens are telling of the glory of God;
And their expanse is declaring the work of His hands.
(Psalm 19:1)

If all that energy is consumed and all the heavens exist simply to shine forth the glory of God, it is no waste; it is energy spent with a purpose. We must grasp the point that the worshiping heart will see the glory of God in that which is truly beautiful. To know beauty does not mean we will know God, but to know God does mean we will want to express His glory beautifully.

A certain woman decided to make an investment in beauty to

express her love for our Lord (Mark 14:3-9). Hers was a beautiful offering to appeal to the sense of smell. She took an alabaster vial of costly perfume of pure nard, broke the vial, and then poured it over His head. Right away the utilitarian, social-action group began to criticize this extravagance—why waste this! It could have been sold and the money given to the poor. Jesus answered in verse 6, *"Let her alone; why do you bother her? She has done a good deed to Me."* Our Lord not only appreciated her investment in beauty in His behalf, He went on to say that (v. 9) *"wherever the gospel is preached in the whole world, that also which this woman has done shall be spoken of in memory of her."* Surely our Lord gives His support to the fact that a properly motivated investment in beauty is no waste; it is a most worthy act of worship!

Wherever possible, and appropriate, our striving for beauty ought to be in earnest. Opulence in the adoration of His name could not be an overstatement. At times, however, just a touch of beauty will add immeasurably to our environment for worship.

The Redwood Empire of Northern California is one of the places on this earth where our Lord has adorned the land with beauty that calls for praise to His name. Not far from Santa Rosa, California, there are several retreats and encampments that take advantage of the great forests, now intermingled with farmlands.

One of these campgrounds is run by the Christian and Missionary Alliance Church. It is called the Alliance Redwoods. There are several substantial and functional buildings on the facility. Each is well built, but rustic in style to fit into the environment.

The basic meeting hall, quaintly called the Tabernacle, would not stand out from any of a large number of retreat meeting halls—except for one thing. There is a touch of beauty in this rustic building that elevates the room as a place truly to worship God.

High in the front of the building, and at times a bit hard to see because of the roof joists, there is a lovely stained glass window that is filled with multiplex biblical symbolism and which brings color, light, and mystery into the room. The building is no longer ordinary, but special. A touch of beauty has sanctified the Tabernacle and has set it apart for special use.[2]

BE A TEMPLE

Christian, consider your call to be a temple. As Paul the Apostle used this metaphor in writing to the Corinthians, it is possible that he was not referring to Solomon's temple; they might not have known the Old Testament that well. They surely knew of the pagan temples to the goddess Diana, for they were prominent on the landscape of their city. Either way, the example has great meaning when it is applied to the believer's call to be a temple.

May we suggest these ways. First, the temple in fulfilling its primary function draws attention to the deity it contains, not to itself! All the splendor, the caretaking, the design, everything about the temple is to draw the onlooker to the indwelling deity. Is that, before God, our position as a temple? God does not share His glory with another. As a temple of God, our appearance, activity, and motivation as an act of worship will draw attention to the hope within us—not to ourselves.

Second, the priests were in the temple to see that it was kept clean. The deity would be offended if there were dirt and pollution; such would be unbecoming to a temple. As believer priests (1 Peter 2:9) Christians are to carry on the continuous temple cleansing. We live in a sin-cursed world which does not help in keeping temples pure. In fact, the media are filled with temple pollutants. But God has provided the means of forgiveness (1 John 1:9) by which the believer priest may see to his temple's appropriate cleanliness. Let us be clean before our God; then His beauty will shine through.

Third, the temple location is always important. Solomon's temple was erected on the historic site of Ornan's threshing floor, a priceless property which David bought for his sacrifice (1 Chronicles 21). The Corinthian temples were located in prominent sites where they could be seen by all in the city. When the populace went about their daily routine they could not help seeing the temple and being reminded of its function. It was there as an object of remembrance. Christian, consider your strategic location in the neighborhood, office, job, school, etc. God has placed you, His temple, in just the place He wants to shed His light, His beauty.

Temples of God are not located by accident, but by sovereign design—consider your location.

In the work of ministry, there is a place for beauty. We are temples of the most high God, designed to draw attention to our God, remain clean and useful for His purposes, and be seen and read of men that they, too, might know Him. Are we beautiful? Can we appreciate beauty? Commit yourself to it.

Chapter 9, Notes

[1]Peter Toon, *Knowing God Through the Liturgy* (Bramcote Notts., Great Britain: Grove Books, 1975), pp. 23-24.

[2]Harry W. Webster, the designer and crafter of the Trinity Window, explains its varied symbolism in a brochure which concludes with the legend: "Trinity Window. Dedicated to the Glory of God, and presented to the Alliance Redwoods in loving memory of our daughter Geneva, 1947-1970."

Part 3

The Aspects of Worship

Chapter 10

Amen to His Glory

"Let the Amen Sound from His People Again . . ."

We suspect that wherever the Gospel has gone, some biblical words have accompanied the Good News into the receiving languages. Among those words of accompaniment is the great biblical term *Amen*. For example, national believers in Honduras likely share very few words with national believers in Indonesia; but one word they both use and enjoy is the word Amen.

Amen is a Hebrew word that is found in both Testaments from the Torah to Revelation. This word is from a root having the meaning, "to be established, to be faithful, to be firm." When we say Amen we are saying, "let it be," or "so be it." Actually, saying Amen is saying "Yes" to God.

On occasion we find the great words of our faith misunderstood or abused. (Did we say "on occasion"?) So it is that the word Amen is used sometimes by people in conversations or in responses where little thought of God might be in view. Sometimes people say Amen when another person states a prejudice or a bias held in common. At times it seems as if the more outlandish the idea is, the stronger comes the shout Amen by a supporter!

AN UNFINISHED PRAYER

When Ron was a young boy he and his family used to watch a weekly musical television program that had one segment of Christian song surrounded by more popular music. The band leader would say a prayer following that song. During the prayer he would often express strong Christian sentiment, but he would never close his prayer with the word "Amen." Even when he would use the words, "we pray in Jesus' name," he would still leave off the Amen.

One day out of exasperation at the unfinished nature of the prayer, Ron wrote a letter to the band leader, Horace Heidt, and asked him to please end his prayers "the way the Bible does" with the word Amen. Mr. Heidt responded in a very gracious letter (which Ron framed), and began this practice the next week. A Christian friend, suitably impressed with the whole affair, suggested (somewhat inappropriately!) that this must be what the Bible means when it says, "and a little child shall lead them"![1]

A prayer without an Amen seems like a sentence without final punctuation. It is like a golf ball left on the lip of the cup and not tapped home. Such a prayer seems unfinished and incomplete to us. Interestingly enough, however, the practice of concluding a prayer with Amen developed in the New Testament period. Great Old Testament prayers lack this word. It is not found, for example, in the prayers of Eliezer the servant of Abraham (Genesis 24:12-14),[2] Hannah (1 Samuel 1:10-11), Daniel (Daniel 9:3-19), Ezra (Ezra 9:5-15), or Nehemiah (Nehemiah 1:4-11, 9:5-38). Amen is found at the end of many prayers in the New Testament (e.g., Ephesians 3:20-21; Philippians 4:20; Revelation 7:12).[3]

We are in full agreement with the Reformers and with the Church in its expansion through the centuries, in hundreds of places and in multiplied hundreds of dialects, that prayer to God ought to end with Amen. What we also wish to assert is that the Bible presents a greater role for the use of Amen than we usually experience. For Amen means more than just that the prayer is finished.

AMEN IN THE OLD TESTAMENT

For readers whose church experience has been in highly structured and formal settings, the suggestion that Christian people ought to shout Amen may raise images of snake-handler revival meetings or exuberant derelicts mumbling in a skid road mission.[4] To such readers we ask that you bear with us.

When we examine the use of Amen in the Old Testament, we find that it is used basically in two ways. One use is a formula by which the people "confirm the validity of an oath and declare themselves ready to bear its consequences."[5] Examples include the twelve oaths of Deuteronomy 27:15-26. One of these reads in the following manner.

The Levites shall say:
"Cursed is he who distorts the justice due an alien, orphan, and widow."

And all the people shall say,
"Amen!"   (Deuteronomy 27:19)

By the word Amen the congregation is saying "Yes" to God, agreeing with the imprecation.

A second use of Amen in the Old Testament is in the context of praise. A splendid example is given in the covenant renewal under Ezra.

Then Ezra blessed Yahweh the great God.
And all the people answered,
   "Amen, Amen!"
while lifting up their hands;
then they bowed low and worshiped Yahweh with their faces to the ground.   (Nehemiah 8:6)

This passage is a touchstone for the use of Amen in congregational worship. By their exultant double Amen the congregation declared its corporate solidarity in the praise of God. Together all the people said "Yes!" to God, agreeing with the sentiment expressed by Ezra in his joy in the Lord.

Similarly in 1 Chronicles 16:8-36 we find the words of a

magnificent psalm of praise to God. The concluding blessing of God in the psalm (v. 36) is followed by the words below.

> *Then all the people said,*
> *"Amen," and praised Yahweh.* (1 Chronicles 16:36b)

The word Amen has been used in the Psalms in the doxologies that conclude each of the first books of hymns. Three of these use the double Amen (Psalms 41:13; 72:19; 89:52). Book Four of the Psalms concludes with a doxology similar to that in 1 Chronicles 16:36.

> *Blessed be Yahweh, the God of Israel,*
> *From everlasting even to everlasting.*
> *And let all the people say,*
>   *"Amen."*
> *Praise Yahweh!*[6]   (Psalm 106:48)

AMEN IN THE NEW TESTAMENT

The response Amen to statements of God's greatness and wonder is given regularly in the New Testament. Writers of the New Testament at times add Amen almost as an incidental in the flow of an argument, but this grand word punctuates the splendor of God. Romans 1:25 illustrates this nicely.

> *For they exchanged the truth of God for a lie, and wor-*
> *shiped and served the creature rather than the Creator,*
> *who is blessed forever. Amen.*

This blessing of God and the assertion Amen are not a central part of Paul's argument here, but these items serve to heighten the enormity of the perversions of wicked men. The One whom they spurn is blessed and adored in the context of their cursing and condemnation.

A more expected use of the word Amen comes at the conclusion of Paul's wonderful doxology on God's wisdom in Romans 11:33-36. The last words reflect the Psalms.

To Him be the glory forever.
Amen.   (Romans 11:36b)

In addition to numerous uses in the Epistles, the word Amen is also found prominently in the Book of Revelation. Amen is used in passages which grant strong assent to the truth of the return of the Lord (1:7; 22:20), in doxological settings (1:6), and in passages descriptive of exuberant worship (5:14; 19:4). On one occasion Amen is used even as a title of our Lord. In His letter to the church in Laodicea, the Lord describes Himself as,

The Amen
the faithful and true Witness,
the Beginning of the creation of God.[7]
                                        (Revelation 3:14)

The worship of God described in Revelation 7 is unforgettable in its comprehensive panorama of personages involved and in the luster of its praise. The great, innumerable multitude of the redeemed *"from every nation and all tribes and peoples and tongues"* join together in great praise to God (vv. 9-10). They are then conjoined by all the angels, the twenty-four elders, and the four living creatures who climax this paean of praise with a blessing framed by a double Amen.

Amen,
blessing and glory and wisdom and thanksgiving
and honor and power and might,
be to our God forever and ever.
Amen!   (Revelation 7:12)

In this panoply of praise the biblical use of Amen is unsurpassed. Saying Amen is saying Yes to God. When we say Amen to His glory, we find ourselves in studied continuity with the redeemed of all ages, of all peoples, and of all places. Indeed, we join the holy angels and the mystical and mysterious personages surrounding the most holy throne of the living God.

Let us then say Amen. We should not trivialize this holy word, but allow it to work its way among our people, joining us together in strong assent to the glory of God.

> Saying "Amen" to God involves a submission to accept the will of God and to commit oneself to the purpose of God. Saying "Amen" means that we are putting ourselves at God's disposal as our ultimate offering to Him.[8]

One way we may use this word is suggested by Robert G. Rayburn. Rather than have the one leading in prayer say Amen at the end of his own prayer, Rayburn says, "let the congregation use it to indicate their hearty agreement with and fellowship in the offering up of the praise and petitions of his prayer."[9]

SING AMEN

How better to respond with vibrant resonance to a great musical statement of truth than to sing a firm Amen with spirit and understanding? To sing it at the end of every hymn would be to rob it of its impact, but never to sing it robs us of a great affirming punctuation. Certain hymns of praise and prayer fairly beg for a solid or somber Amen, while for many other songs of Christian expression (or sentiment) the word would be excess baggage.

Some of the new, more skillfully edited hymnals have been selective in their placement of final Amens. A few years ago, one could tell a "fundamental" song book from a liberal hymnal at a glance; the Amens were printed everywhere in the latter and were not to be found in the former. Better thinking and planning are evident in a few of our newer hymnals today, however.

The familiar hymn "Crown Him With Many Crowns" *(Diademata)* is one which should probably be sung with the congregational Amen. It makes a strong and significant statement with regard to the person of Christ, His life, His peace, His love, His redemption, His eternity, His glory, etc.; every redeemed soul should be so full of exuberance at the end of such a statement that a hearty Amen would follow as naturally as one breath follows another. A soft hymn of dedication and devotion like "Something For Thee" sung at a lower volume but with great contrition needs a humble Amen for its finish, for it is a fervent prayer. Leaders sensitive to the Holy Spirit, the sense of the song, and the significance of the moment need to consider exactly when to or not to sing Amen; but do not avoid it!

If a church choir seldom sings an anthem (or selection) which "demands" an Amen, they are missing the privilege and excitement of a most thrilling moment. Composers traditional and contemporary have made great use of Amen to place the crowning glory on great expressions of praise, statements about the ultimate victory and glory of God.

Consider the *Messiah* by George Frederick Handel. Most of us know the major choruses from that masterpiece, the "Hallelujah Chorus," "For Unto Us a Child Is Born," etc.; but too few are the church performances of this spiritually and musically stellar work which end as the composer intended with the glorious Amen which follows "Worthy Is the Lamb That Was Slain." After spending countless notes and marvelous melodic, harmonic, and rhythmic devices to express the meaning of the life and work of our Lord from the early prophecy of the Old Testament to the final victory seen by John in Revelation, the composer turns to the most biblical response of Amen. The choir sings nothing but that single word for six pages, not because it could not be heard or understood the first time, but because it requires that length to add the final touch of "*yes*, God, we agree; *yes*, God, we recognize how great You really are; *yes*, God, we are with You; *yes*, God, we are rejoicing in being heirs of God and joint heirs with Jesus Christ." Listen to that Amen, and allow it to sink in; you will never be the same!

A CRACK OF THUNDER

Choral settings of the Amen are often most appropriate and have served the Church well. These settings are especially fitting following words of blessing and adoration of God. But the unison congregational response to the praise of God in a hearty, audible Amen is unsurpassed. It can be like a "crack of thunder," as Jerome described its use in the churches of his day.[10]

Amen is not a trivial word, coming randomly from a few

hyper participants in the "Amen-corner." It is instead a noble term for all of the congregation to use as we glorify God together. Paul wrote these words describing the ultimate mystery of the *Amen*.

> *For as many as may be the promises of God,*
> *in Him they are yes;*
> *wherefore also by Him is our Amen*
> *to the glory of God through us.*
>
> (2 Corinthians 1:20)

Just as in Christ the promises of God are affirmed ("in Him they are yes"), by Christ we are able to say Amen to the glory of God.

Chapter 10, Notes

[1]These words from Isaiah 11:6 are perhaps among the most often misused words of Isaiah.

[2]It may be, however, that a wag would note from verse 15 that Abraham's servant had not quite finished his prayer.

[3]The word Amen may be a later addition to the text in some places, e.g., Matthew 6:13; Philippians 4:23; Colossians 4:18. The reader of the King James or New King James Bible will see this word in some passages where it is lacking in the New American Standard Bible or the New International Version.

[4]Often misspelled "skid row," "skid road" is the genuine Northwest contribution to American language in which some local writers take misguided pride.

[5]Ludwig Koehler and Walter Baumgartner, *Lexicon in Veteris Testamenti Libros*, 2nd ed. (Leiden: E. J. Brill, 1958), p. 61.

[6]The five-book schema of the Book of Psalms is described in Ronald Barclay Allen, *Praise! A Matter of Life and Breath* (Nashville: Thomas Nelson, 1980), pp. 98-106.

[7]The Old Testament may also use "Amen" as a name for Deity in Isaiah 65:16,
He who invokes a blessing on himself in the land
    shall do so by the God whose name is Amen,
and he who utters an oath in the land
    shall do so by the God of Amen (NEB).

[8]Robert W. Bailey, *New Ways in Christian Worship* (Nashville: Abingdon, 1981), p. 20.

[9]Robert G. Rayburn, *O Come, Let Us Worship: Corporate Worship in the Evangelical Church* (Grand Rapids: Baker Book House, 1980), p. 151. He also speaks of unison "Amens" punctuating prayers of petition, where the one praying pauses for the congregation to express its agreement and assent after each item (pp. 200-201).

[10]Ibid., p. 150.

Chapter 11

The Body of the Believer in Worship

"With Hearts and Hands and Voices . . ."

*O*ur emphasis in this book is steadfastly centered on the state of the inner man and the inner woman when believers gather together as a community to worship the living God. Heart worship is God's desire in every aspect of our living, both personally and corporately.

It may then seem to be somewhat out of place for us to deal with the physical body of the worshiper as she or he participates in the community. When we think of physical actions, we likely find ourselves picturing what we have learned to describe as ritual actions or emotional excesses. "Excesses" like clapping or lifting one's hands toward the heavens. Or "ritual actions" like bowing and kneeling, or bending low one's body. "These are the things others might do, not me," our minds think. We need to look inward at this point, however, before becoming too critical. Some of the motions considered excessive may be biblical.

WE DON'T DO THAT

For worshipers in many churches today, there are few opportunities for any physical bodily action in worship except for sitting. No one opposes standing while singing some of the hymns, but on occasion it appears that this simply allows people to adjust their frames before the sermon begins. Raising the hands seems to be too emotional an act; bending the knees is too formal. These actions are foreign to us.

A friend of ours on one occasion was describing an encounter he had had with a woman who goes to a charismatic church in our city. She asked him if people raise their hands in his (non-charismatic) church. He responded that they did not. She then probed him as to why they refrained from what the Psalms speak of doing in worship services. My friend's defensive reaction was that this whole idea seemed pretty silly. "Perhaps the Psalms do speak of such actions, but we don't do them. Why should we? Just because a pastor tells us to do so?" My friend's response seems to suggest that habit and precedent are the arbiters of actions; that custom (*my* custom) settles issues. "That is not a custom of ours. Why should we do it?"

WITH MY BODY

But what about physical actions in worship? Does custom dictate action, or are there biblical principles that can guide us with clarity and authority in making our decisions in this area?

One of the delightful elements in the older Anglican wedding is the clause, "With my body I thee worship." In these words one lover says to another:

> My body will adore you,
> and your body alone will I cherish.
> I will with my body declare your worth.

Similarly, the Scriptures give us ample warrant to suggest that with our bodies we may adore the glory of God. Heart worship and body worship are not mutually exclusive; they complement each other. Peter E. Gillquist states the basis of the issue.

> To tie it all together—we simply can't be spiritual without being physical. For man was never created to be either *just* a soul or *just* a body. We are not one or the

other, but *both* (his emphasis).[1]

A moment's thought will help us to remember the physical aspects of our worship quite apart from bodily posture. The two most basic institutions of our corporate worship life are physical actions. The practice of baptism is a physical act, regardless of how much water might be used in a given congregation. The celebration of the Lord's Table is a most basic physical action. Further, we know of some communions where the washing of one another's feet is also done as a community act of worship.

Hence, even apart from the issue of posture we find that our worship experiences are marked by physical actions. Finally, we could not even have a corporate worship service without the presence of our physical bodies. This is the subtle (?) danger of the electronic church. Watching a worship service on television may be an act signally blessed by God for a given individual, but that physical separation from the community is a serious loss. It is not insignificant to be away from one's fellowship (see again Psalm 42).

And with My Hands

Psalm 28 beautifully blends worship of "heart and hands and voices." In David's prayer to God for mercy, he says:

> *Hear my cry for mercy*
> *as I call to you for help,*
> *as I lift up my hands*
> *toward your Most Holy Place.*   (v. 2, NIV)

Here we see his words of petition conjoined to his action of lifting his hands as a suppliant, expecting mercy to come from the God whose mercy is revealed in the Most Holy Place. Later in this same poem, David finds that God's great grace has been extended to him another time. Now heart and voice conjoin in exultation.

> *Yahweh is my strength and my shield;*
> *my heart trusts in him, and I am helped.*
> *My heart leaps for joy*

and I will give thanks to him in song.   (v. 7, NIV)

The *heart* in the Old Testament is a word often used to describe the inner being of an individual. The *hand* is a convenient symbol for the physical body. Artists throughout the ages have recognized in the human hand one of the most difficult features of the anatomy to portray well. Animators, for example, often reduce the number of digits on their characters because of the complexity of the hand. The hand is not only complex in its structure, but it is marvelously expressive of personality. Is it not for this reason that we read so often of the "hand of the Lord"? By the visual image of His hand extended in mercy or clenched in wrath, we draw more closely to the experience of the reality of the God who is Spirit.

HAND AND SPIRIT

It is the human hand which beautifully typifies the human spirit. It is distinct from the hands of the lower animals in appearance and dexterity. Observe the hands of a skilled person; no matter the field, it is an amazing exhibition of the genius of our creative Lord. Think of the fingers of the typist, the seamstress, the potter, the painter, the violinist, the mechanic, the builder; the list could be endless. The hand allows the creative to be expressive; it can do so much good or evil. The hand can be firm, as a parent's spank or firm grasp; it can be gentle, stroking the hair or face of a child or lover.

Once Gordon was giving piano instructions to a highly skilled surgeon. The doctor was skilled well beyond many of his peers in some of the most delicate surgical procedures, but his skillful hands were not doing so well on a keyboard. They began to discuss physiological reasons for his musical difficulties. (It is Gordon's view that musical motor skills must be learned early, before the late teens, if one ever expects to be a skilled instrumentalist.)

The doctor soon became the teacher as he began to rhapsodize and be filled with ecstasy over the marvel of the human hand. He had recently done major repair work on a severely injured hand in the emergency room, and he was once again impressed and full of praise to God for His design displayed in our "fearfully and wonderfully made" hands. He said, "I don't see how ANYBODY could be an atheist and objectively study the design of a hand. Certainly God did much to verify His glory in that one creative act."[2]

I SPREAD OUT MY HANDS

For the Old Testament believers, and for the first Christians of the New Testament period, the raising of one's hands to the Lord was a regular part of worship. We see two basic functions in raising one's hands. In prayer a petitioner expects that God in His great grace will respond to his request. With hands extended, the believer postures his or her faith: God *will* respond to those who stretch out to His mercy.

An example of the use of extended hands in prayer of petition was given in Psalm 28:2 (above). Another is found in Psalm 88:9b,

I call to you, O Yahweh, every day;
I spread out my hands to you.   (NIV)

As we think on the concept of outstretched hands, the imagery suggested is complex. One holds out his hands to receive a gift of God's grace. But the extension of the open hand is also suggestive of a lack of duplicity, deceit, or guile. We do not come with our hands closed, expressive of secret desires or hostile intentions, indicative of the opposite thing that we are saying. We come rather with our hands open, our desires made known, and our expectancy demonstrated by our reverent position.

We can see a second function in raising one's hands to the Lord in contexts of praise to His greatness. Psalm 134:1-2 is illustrative of this practice by the worship leaders in the congregation:

Praise Yahweh, all you servants of Yahweh
    who minister by night in the house of Yahweh.
Lift up your hands in the sanctuary
    and praise Yahweh.   (NIV)

The congregation as well as the worship leaders would lift their hands in praise to God. Observe Nehemiah 8:6.

> *Then Ezra blessed Yahweh the great God.*
> *And all the people answered,*
>   *"Amen, Amen!" while lifting up their hands;*
> *then they bowed low and worshiped Yahweh*
>   *with their faces to the ground.*

We should resist the temptation to say that this practice is merely an Old Testament concept, divorced from the New Testament. One wearies of hearing biblical concepts dismissed by such a cavalier approach to truth. For example, in a recent letter to the editor of a West Coast daily, one reader spoke disparagingly of a similar editorial concept as reflecting "a pre-Christian, primitive view of the Old Testament prophets," and not something for the Christian (or the modern). As a matter of fact, the "pre-Christian, primitive views" in that instance are reinstated by the New Testament writers. The same is true for raising of one's hands in prayer. Paul wrote about this subject to Timothy.

> *I want men everywhere to lift up holy hands in prayer,*
> *without anger or disputing.*   (1 Timothy 2:8, NIV)

The raising of one's hands in prayer or in praise to God then is neither a new phenomenon developed within churches bent toward the emotional nor is it a holdover from the pre-Christian era. Rather, this practice is thoroughly biblical, having been practiced in the worship patterns of the Old Testament period, and carried on into the New Testament era—and therefore into the Christian era.

IN BENEDICTION

The practice of closing a worship service by words of benediction spoken with raised hands is possibly patterned after the account of our Lord in His ascension into heaven. Luke records this in his narrative.

> *When he had led them out to the vicinity of Bethany,*
> *he lifted up his hands and blessed them.*

*While he was blessing them, he left them and was taken
up into heaven.* (Luke 24:50-51, NIV)

Gillquist comments on this testimony.

The last glimpse the disciples had of our Lord Jesus
Christ was as He was ascending to the Father with
hands lifted on high! As their mediator, soon to be
crowned High King of heaven, He returned to the
Father with hands lifted, interceding for those He loved
and blessing them.[3]

It should be altogether appropriate for the worship leader in
today's congregation to give the words of benediction with outstretched hands in imitation of Christ.

We need to find ways within our worship services physically
to raise our hands in prayer and in praise to God. We do not make
this suggestion to be sensational, bizarre, or new and different.
The Church is weary with books presenting new truths. This is not
new truth, however. It is as old as our faith. We find ample biblical
precept and precedent to encourage us to grow in this area.

Listen to the words of Anne Ortlund.

Variations in posture? Wouldn't it be glorious if we
were free enough in our inhibitions to stand, sit, or
kneel as our individual hearts required, lifting arms or
not, eyes closed to all around, but ears and hearts
opened to heaven?!

As Solomon finished his prayer in 2 Chronicles 7:1, fire
came out of heaven and all the people fell flat on the
pavement.

Words fail me.[4]

WITH HOLY HANDS

Hands can be raised wrongly to the Lord, of course. God
spoke through Isaiah excoriating the people of Jerusalem who were
in the proper posture, but who were not acting from a proper heart.

> So when you spread out your hands in prayer,
> I will hide My eyes from you,
> Yes, even though you multiply prayers,
> I will not listen.
>   Your hands are covered with blood.   (Isaiah 1:15)

The larger portion of Isaiah 1:11-15 suggests that it is possible to do all the right things but to do nothing right—if the heart is not right before the Lord. It is *holy* hands we raise to the Lord (1 Timothy 2:8) to bless His holy name and to implore His matchless grace. Bloody hands are pictures of soiled lives. Mistreatment of the poor, abuse of the unfortunate, debasing of the things of God, even bloodshed—such are the marks God sees on hands that are raised to Him when those hands are not holy.

On the other hand (pun intended), when one's life is lived in testimony to the grace of God, when one's inner being is at peace with God, when one's heart is throbbing with the joy of God, then the lifting of the hands will be most salutary. God's words in Isaiah 1:15 are condemnatory not of this action of worship, but of the attitude of the worshipers. God has not condemned the act of raising one's hands any more than He has canceled the act of prayer. Occasionally in informal retreat settings, we have encouraged people to raise their hands in praise or in prayer. On each occasion, even though some people had feelings of unfamiliar settings or awkward circumstances, none has yet broken out in a rash or turned green!

At issue is always what the Bible teaches, not what we might have learned through custom, hearing, or imagination. Recently Ron found himself in an intense debate on the doctrine of Scripture in a coffee shop. A young woman joined the discussion and presented a novel idea that lacked any foundation in fact and in Scripture. When she was asked her authority for such a point of view, the woman responded, "the Bible says it." She did not know where the Bible said such a thing, but she was "sure it was there."

One might similarly state that in a given issue of *Time* magazine there was the following report: The initial issues in the strike of the air traffic control personnel were prompted by their union leaders' dislike of a certain green parfait served in the restaurant of the Dulles Airport in Washington, D.C. Only a reading of the *Time* article in question would settle the issue as to whether such a statement in fact was made or even alleged. All manner of absurdities have been claimed to occur in the Bible with no more evidence than that of green parfait in the Dulles Airport.

The Bible is not a marshmallow fluff or cotton candy. It is true that some passages have been subjected to widely varying interpretations, but there is still an objective meaning and reality to even the most elusive texts. When the Bible speaks plainly about issues of worship, those clear statements are considerably more important than one's feelings or customs or likes and dislikes.

On Bended Knee

Not only does the Bible encourage us at times to raise our hands in prayer and praise, it also bids us to kneel in adoration of our great God.

It is not generally known that the primary Old Testament word for "worship" is a word that basically means "to make oneself prostrate." This Hebrew verb, *hawah* (given as *shahah* in the older dictionaries), is found in the Old Testament in a rare verbal formation termed causative-reflexive. That is, while standard translations simply use the word "worship" for this verb (e.g., Psalm 29:2b in NASB, NIV, RSV, etc.), a more expansive definition might be: "make yourselves to lie prostrate (before Yahweh)." Such physical actions of submission before the Lord are found in the New Testament on a number of occasions. One of these is given in Ephesians 3:14, *"For this cause I bow my knees unto the Father of our Lord Jesus Christ"* (KJV).

The act of bowing, kneeling, or prostrating oneself is designed to be an outward symbol of an inward attitude of gratitude, submission, and humility.

In the lovely pastoral book of Ruth we find a splendid example. Chapter 2 describes the valiant Boaz acting toward Ruth, the alien widow, with such grace that she found herself quite overwhelmed. As a destitute young widow, and a foreigner as well, Ruth had slim prospects for kindness in her new land. This is particularly likely as we remember that the story of the book is set in the time of the judges, when biblical piety and social concern were rarely expressed.[5]

But Ruth found her every need met by Boaz. Not only was she allowed to glean in his field; she was told by him not to go to any other field but his. His men were commanded to allow her to glean among the cut sheaves, and they were even ordered to drop grain surreptitiously from the sheaves they had bundled so that she might gather among that as well. Moreover, at meal time Ruth was invited to eat with Boaz's workers, and he personally gave her delicacies from his table.

Ruth's response to the initial words of Boaz in these great actions of grace was one of incredulity.

> Then she fell on her face, bowing to the ground *and said to him,*
> > *"Why have I found favor in your sight*
> > *that you should take notice of me,*
> > *since I am a foreigner?"*   (Ruth 2:10)

In her physical action of bowing low before Boaz, Ruth was displaying outwardly her tremendous inner sense of gratitude, wonder, and astonishment.

CULTURE AND CUSTOM

As we read the story of Ruth, we recognize full well that bowing and prostrating oneself are actions that were a part of ancient Near Eastern culture, and that they are not actions that we usually display in our North American (or Northern European) culture.

Peoples *do* differ, both nationally and individually, both culturally and ethnically. Frank Baxter describes a certain stuffy Briton saying something "was not without interest." Then, so that his American audience would appreciate the intensity of this seemingly casual remark, Dr. Baxter suggests that for a certain type of Englishman to say something is "not without interest," is the equivalent of saying there was "a Frenchman dancing in the streets with garlands in his hair."[6]

When people do things that are nice for us—even extraordinarily nice—we probably do not respond in the way that Ruth did by groveling on the ground.

Nevertheless, kneeling before the LORD is a trans-cultural issue. To kneel before the Lord is not an act descriptive only of a quaint custom done by a foreign woman in an isolated village from ancient biblical times. On one day, all peoples everywhere will kneel before the Lord of glory.

The well-known words of Philippians 2:5-6 describe the humiliation of the Lord Jesus Christ in His incarnation, an example of the humility His people ought to have before one another (Philippians 2:1-5). This superb passage climaxes in a grand manner that is comprehensive of God's will for all creatures of all ages in all places:

> *that at the name of Jesus*
>   every knee should bow,
> *of those who are in heaven,*
>   *and on earth,*
>   *and under the earth,*
> *and that every tongue should confess*
>   *that Jesus Christ is Lord,*
>   *to the glory of God the Father.*
>
>   (Philippians 2:10-11)

In these words the biblical end of mankind is stated: the goal of the Incarnation is the exaltation of the Lord Jesus Christ to the glory of God the Father. And the end of man in this regard is public confession on *bended knee*.

You see, the question really is not "Shall we kneel or not in our worship of God and of His Christ?" We shall one day all kneel. The question is, rather, "Shall we who *will* kneel in the future, kneel *now* as well?"

The words of Philippians 2:10, 11, are also paralleled in Romans 14:11, where we learn (if we missed it earlier), that the kneeling confession of God by all humanity is a trans-Testamental issue. Paul says in Romans 14:11,

For it is written,
   "As I live, says the LORD.
      every knee shall bow to Me,
         and every tongue shall give praise to God."

The passage that Paul quotes in saying "it is written" is Isaiah 45:23.

"I have sworn by Myself,
   the word has gone forth
      from My mouth in righteousness
And will not turn back,
   that to Me every knee will bow,
      every tongue will swear allegiance."

Here is not an idle word in an obscure backwater text (if there is such a thing!). Here is an issue so sure, so certain, and so central that Old and New Testament writers seem to outdo each other in its proclamation. The very character of God is at issue. He has sworn by His own being; the word is out, it is righteous, it is certain, it will not return empty.

THEN LET US KNEEL

Since we shall all kneel before Him, why are some of us so hesitant to kneel in worship today? Where the Scriptures speak clearly we ought to obey and act with certainty. Where the Scriptures are oblique, indirect, or shrouded in cultural overtones, we may make more personal and individual decisions.

Anglican believers kneel before the Lord—so ought Baptist believers. Lutheran believers kneel before the Lord—so ought Evangelical Free believers. Greek Orthodox believers kneel before the Lord—so ought Free Methodist believers. Those of us in free church traditions should examine our evangelical practices in the light of the Scripture with the same measure of diligence that we use in determining and supporting our evangelical faith.

We certainly do not wish to imply that all of our praying needs to be done on our knees. Here, too, we call for balance. Perfectly acceptable—and biblical—positions for prayer include standing and sitting.

What we do wish to say is that kneeling is a fitting congregational symbol of "humility, vulnerability, and dependence" before God.[7]

The two principal objections some might present to the ideas of raising one's hands and bending one's knees in evangelical worship services are:

> 1. These are just cultural factors found in the biblical world which the Bible describes but does not prescribe; and
>
> 2. God's interest is in our heart attitude, not in our physical posture, for our physical actions can too easily become mechanical and hypocritical.

It might be that *behind* these two objections there are some more personal issues, alluded to before: (1) *We* don't do these things in our church, and (2) *I* would be uncomfortable in doing them. The real reasons are known only by you.

THE HEART AND THE ACT

We have attempted to defuse the objection to hand-raising and kneeling stemming from cultural reasons by marking out texts which not only describe but which also prescribe physical actions in worship. Furthermore, some of these texts speak in universal, trans-cultural terms. These are not just cultural items we may shrug away casually by saying "we don't do them."

The second objection about mechanical actions which lack heart motivations has more merit and calls for a closer look. In our present study we repeatedly observe that the heart attitude must be central in any act of worship. We are to *"draw near with a sincere heart in full assurance of faith"* (Hebrews 10:22).

But a right heart attitude does not exclude physical action. Imagine a young man who is physiologically sound, but who never embraces his wife, even though there is no reason not to. He might say that his love for his wife is given only by a great heart attitude, but not by physical actions. We may surmise that such a marriage will not last nor will it be a happy one! Absence or illness or any number of circumstances may hinder physical embraces temporarily in a good marriage. But the marriage is not likely to last long if touch willfully is neglected.

We are not simply spirit beings. We are more than hearts or souls or "inner beings." We are persons possessing an intricate complex of physical and spiritual realities. We who worship God truly with the heart, do so with our physical bodies as well.

We err if we think that merely by doing an act we will necessarily be different, posture being a means to the end of worship. We may often find that the outward act might well lead to an inward reality. Eugene H. Peterson explains this in commenting on Psalm 134 with its command to lift up one's hands.

> We are invited to bless the Lord; we are commanded to bless the Lord. And then someone says, "But I don't feel like it. And I won't be a hypocrite. I can't bless the Lord if I don't feel like blessing the Lord. It wouldn't be honest."

> The biblical response to that is, "Lift up your hands to the holy place, and bless the LORD!" You can lift up your hands regardless of how you feel; it is a simple motor movement. You may not be able to command your heart, but you can command your arms. Lift your arms in blessing, just maybe your heart will get the message and be lifted up also in praise. We are psychosomatic beings; body and spirit are intricately interrelated. Go through the motions of blessing God and your spirit will pick up the cue and follow along. "For why do men lift their hands when they pray? Is it not that their hearts may be raised at the same time to God?"[8]

If we always waited until we felt like worshiping, we might not worship at all. We simply do not jump out of bed every Sunday morning shouting "Hallelujah, today we get to worship the living God!" There are likely some Sunday mornings in which we barely make it to church at all. But there are times among those "down" mornings when we are surprised by the grace of God and we find ourselves worshiping in spirit and truth. That would not have happened if we had not first got our bodies in motion.

Objections to changing one's posture in worship are the same types of objections that might be leveled against just about any Christian virtue. Witnessing, giving, acts of Christian charity could all be done with the wrong attitude—selfishly, rather than from the heart. Any Christian virtue may begin grooming itself in the boudoir of human carnality.

Until the return of the Lord there will always be those who try to give the appearance of truth, but who do not live it. The Pharisee who prayed self-righteously (Luke 18:10-14) had the complete list of correct physical actions. The publican that our Lord contrasted with that Pharisee shied from even looking toward heaven. And who was correct? As Ken Medema has paraphrased: The one worshiped God, and the other merely rumpled his clothing.[9]

Nevertheless, negative examples do not alter the standard pattern. We may act wrongly, but act we must, in a combined unification of spirit and action. We pray that God will act through us for His own glory.

PRAISE, NOT PENANCE

One more misconception is noteworthy. Once when Ron was speaking to a friend about the idea of installing kneeling pews in church, the friend responded approvingly about the idea of kneeling, but not on padded rails. "If we are going to kneel," he said, "it should hurt!"

This not-too-uncommon approach to kneeling in worship we believe to be in error. The purpose of kneeling before the Lord is not to increase our pain or discomfort. Nor is it to cause greater difficulty for people with arthritis or poor circulation. Kneeling is supposed to give an outward expression of an inward reality of humility and gratitude toward our majestic God. It is an act of the heart physically expressed.

A few years ago Ron was in Mexico City and he visited the Shrine of the Virgin, Our Lady of Guadalupe. It was Easter week and the plaza before that church was filled with people; supplicants and tourists thronged together indiscriminantly. Unforgettable impressions were made on me by some elderly women who were making their way from one end of the broad plaza to the church on bended knees. Little boys walked beside them, putting cloths in front of them to ease the harsh, penitential movement of knees on the hard, stone surface. Some knees were bleeding, yet these ladies kept on, slowly and painfully. It reminded me of Luther ascending church steps on his knees in Rome before his conversion. Against such touching, but misdirected, actions we protest—with compassion.

We are not arguing for penance, but for praise; we are not calling for pain, but for pleasure as the congregation delights in honoring God *with hearts and voices and even our very bodies.*

Chapter 11, Notes

[1]Gillquist, *The Physical Side of Being Spiritual* (Grand Rapids: Zondervan, 1979), p. 152.

[2]The hand is discussed in terms of God's great creation by Paul Brand and Philip Yancey, *Fearfully and Wonderfully Made* (Grand Rapids: Zondervan, 1980), pp. 161-165.

[3]Gillquist, *The Physical Side of Being Spiritual*, p. 121.

[4]Anne Ortlund, *Up With Worship* (Glendale: Regal Books, Gospel Light Publishers, 1975), p. 78.

[5]Judges 21:25 summarizes that time period in this way: "In those days there was no king in Israel; everyone did what was right in his own eyes." A reading of the Book of Judges simply does not prepare us for the beauty of piety in the Book of Ruth. The righteousness of Boaz is utterly remarkable; the age was desperately evil.

[6]Frank C. Baxter, "The Nature of Poetry." Recorded lecture. New Rochelle: Spoken Arts, Inc., [n.d.] (S.A. 703).

[7]Grady Hardin, *The Leadership of Worship* (Nashville: Abingdon, 1980), p. 61.

[8]Eugene H. Peterson, *A Long Obedience in the Same Direction: Discipleship in an Instant Society* (Downers Grove, Ill.: Inter-Varsity Press, 1980), p. 188. The last two sentences are quoted from John Calvin's *Commentary on the Psalms* (Grand Rapids: Eerdmans, 1949), V, 168.

[9]Ken Medema, "Mr. Simon." This haunting song concludes:
"Two men walked into the church upon that Sunday morn;
  One left slightly wrinkled,
  the other left reborn."
    © Word Music, ASCAP. Used by permission.

Chapter 12

Public Reading of the Scriptures

"Beautiful Words, Wonderful Words,
Wonderful Words of Life."

We are often weakest where we should be the strongest. If anything should go well in our worship services, it is the reading
of the Scriptures. After all, we would die for the right to read our
Bibles in public or in private, but sometimes we hardly make an effort to read the Scriptures well. Some pastors who study hard to
prepare their messages, laboring long over the words of the text, do
not read the same words in a manner befitting their labor and their
hearers' attention.

There may be two reasons for a generally poor showing in the
area of reading the Scriptures in public. On the one hand, we are
accustomed to think in terms of preliminaries and sermon; on the
other hand, we do not stress sufficiently that the reading of God's
Word is itself an act of worship.

An overused term that should be dropped from the vocabu-
lary of worship is the term *preliminaries*. We dump many 'tems
into this lackluster, catch-all term that ought to be major elements
of congregational worship. Music and offerings, reading and praying are not the preliminaries to the "main event" (the sermon).
They are not just things one sits through to warm up for the head-
liner. They are integral elements of worship itself. By perpetuating
the use of the word preliminaries, we are continuing to minimize

and to downplay those things which we should maximize.

When the Word of God *is* read well, we worship Him. The act of reading is an act of worship. Consider again the account of the revival led by Ezra, recorded in Nehemiah 8. In this story we read how the people of Jerusalem gathered together and asked Ezra to bring out the scroll of the Torah, the books of Moses, to read to all the people.

There in the street near the Water Gate of the city, Ezra read the Scripture,

> *from early morning until midday,*
> *in the presence of men and women,*
> > *those who could understand;*
> > *and all the people were attentive*
> > > *to the book of the law.*   (Nehemiah 8:3b)

Ezra was standing on an elevated platform so that he might be seen and heard by all of the people. Standing beside him in a symbolic gesture of support and assent were thirteen worthies, six on one side and seven on the other. When he opened the scroll, all of the people stood up to hear his words. As we have noted in an earlier section, Ezra then blessed the Lord and the congregation responded with a double "Amen," with their hands uplifted. Then the people bowed their heads and prostrated themselves on the ground in adoration of Yahweh.

The Scriptures were read to an intensely attentive congregation. Not only were the words read, they were interpreted and made understandable to the people by several associates of Ezra.

> *And they read from the book,*
> > *from the law of God,*
> > > *translating to give the sense*
> > > *so that they understood the reading.*   (v.8)

The response of the people—weeping. Why? It is possible that the reading of the Torah had presented a strong conviction of sin and of unworthiness before the Lord. It is also possible that the weeping was for joy. For at last they had heard the words of God. Ezra and his associates encouraged the people not to weep nor to mourn, but to exult:

> *"This day is holy to Yahweh your God;*
> *do not mourn or weep."*   (v. 9b)

Instead of weeping, they were to feast; instead of mourning, they were to rejoice. The day was a holy day to the living God. The people were told:

> *neither be ye sorry;*
> *for the joy of Yahweh is your strength.*   (v. 10c, KJV)

In a happy mood the people ate; in joy they drank; with delight they shared food with those who had none,

> *because they understood the words*
> *which had been made known to them.*   (v. 12b)

Truly the reading of the Word of God in a way that is understandable to the people is in itself a supreme act of worship.[1]

OUR LORD'S READING OF THE SCRIPTURE

The public reading of the Hebrew Scripture continued in Jewish worship. This is attested in the gospel account of our Lord reading from the scroll of Isaiah in the synagogue at Nazareth. Luke describes this typical occurrence of public reading which in this case turned out quite extraordinarily (4:16-22). Jesus came to His home town of Nazareth and,

> *as was His custom,*
> *He entered the synagogue on the Sabbath,*
> *and stood up to read.*   (v. 16)

We surmise that the public reading of the Scriptures was an honor here afforded our Lord by the leaders of the synagogue. By God's providence, they handed to the Lord Jesus the scroll of the great prophet Isaiah. He opened the scroll to the passage beginning

at chapter 61. What a moment that must have been, when the Lord
of Scripture was reading to His friends and neighbors the stunning
words of Messianic portent:

> *"The Spirit of the Lord Yahweh is upon me,*
> *Because Yahweh has anointed me*
>   *To bring good news to the afflicted;*
> *He has sent me to bind up the brokenhearted,*
>   *To proclaim liberty to captives,*
>   *And freedom to prisoners;*
> *To proclaim the favorable year of Yahweh,"*
>
>   (Isaiah 61:1-2a)

And there, in the middle of a Hebrew verse, in mid-stride, our Lord
ceased the reading!

What happened next does not directly relate to public reading; but it amplifies our point. In the middle of the Scripture segment for the day, He rewound the scroll and carefully gave the precious text back to the attendant. Then He sat down. Every eye in
the assembly was upon Him. All must have wondered why He
would stop in the middle of such a text; all must have leaned for-
ward to hear what He might have to say. Finally He spoke.

> *"Today this Scripture*
>   *has been fulfilled in your hearing."*   (Luke 4:21)

If ever the reading of the Scripture were a time for worship, certainly this was the time! The One who was the fulfillment of the
promises of the Messiah had just read central words describing His
own Person and the age He now set into process. The Kingdom
could not be far off, when the King was reading self-attesting
Scripture in their presence.

But those neighbors of Jesus did not worship Him; neither did
they worship God. At first they spoke kindly of Him, not really
realizing the import of the declaration He made. As He then began
to make the issue clear, they finally saw the direction of the words
of the Lord. At that point they were enraged. They seized Him,
then pushed and buffeted Him along until they had Him on the
brow of a hill from which they desired to cast Him down to kill Him

for the blasphemy they imagined Him to have spoken. Luke records:

> *But passing through their midst,*
> *He went His way.* (v. 30)

This was neither the time nor the manner of the Lord's death. He was in complete control: "He went His way." We read these words of the synagogue service, and wonder what might have happened if the people of Nazareth had listened to the words of Jesus and had understood the fact that He was indeed the Anointed One of the prophet Isaiah's text. That occasion of Scripture reading would have led to the most significant time of worship in the lives of any of the people assembled there. The very *least* we may observe in our reading of this text is that the Lord considered the public reading of the Scripture a most serious act.

OUR READING OF THE SCRIPTURE

In Paul's first letter to Timothy, the older apostle gave instructions to the young minister concerning the ministry that the Lord desired him to have. Among the instructions that Paul stressed were the following words.

> *Until I come,*
> *devote yourself to the public reading of Scripture,*
> *to preaching and to teaching.*
> (1 Timothy 4:13, NIV)

In Paul's letter to the church at Colossae, he concluded with a similar injunction.

> *After this letter has been read to you,*
> *see that it is also read in the church of the Laodiceans*
> *and that you in turn read the letter from Laodicea.*[2]
> (Colossians 4:16, NIV)

In these two passages we find that the practice of the public reading of Scripture, a standard element in Jewish worship, was also to be a regular part of Christian worship as well. The Scripture is to be used for preaching and teaching (1 Timothy 4:13; 2 Timothy 4:2; Colossians 1:28-29); it is also to be read. We may presume that it is to be read, and read well. What we are reading are the oracles of God!

Those who read the Scriptures in the public assembly should practice their texts aloud. Stumbling over unfamiliar names, mispronouncing words, careless diction, and sloppy speech patterns not only cause the congregation embarrassment (and the reader!); these faults detract from the worship of God that the reading should afford.

Reading that is worship takes place when the reader plans to do well. Good reading of the Scripture is as likely to occur spontaneously as is good preaching—in other words, it doesn't. Reading that is worship may be done in a variety of ways, but planning and preparation are essential in each instance for it to be done well.

In churches which follow the lectionary system, the texts are selected for each week of the church year. Usually there are passages from the Old Testament, from the Epistles, and from the Gospels. In such churches there seems hardly to be an excuse for the reading to be done poorly. The planning has been done; all one needs to do is to practice, and then to read.

In churches which do not follow a charted system of public reading from the Bible, there is at once more liberty in selection—but more room for things to go wrong. One would expect that in a church where the pastor is preaching expositional messages from the Bible, the texts of his messages would usually be the ones selected for public reading. It may well be, however, that the nature of the passage for the morning sermon does not lend itself readily for public reading as worship. Or the text for the sermon may be quite brief, and a longer section might be desired for the public reading. Whatever the circumstances, the texts for reading ought to be selected with care with the purpose of the service in mind and with the worship of God in view.

PARTICIPATION

A challenge ever before those who plan for corporate worship is *participation*. How can we move the congregant from the level of sitter/hearer to participator/doer? Can we corporately model the admonition of James to be a doer as well as a hearer of the word? We would not be so simplistic as to suggest that if one participates in corporate worship (as in reading aloud or praying with a neighbor), that he will then naturally be involved in the other areas of ministry. It does seem clear, though, that the corporate setting is a good place of beginning and encouragement.

A major concern is the lament stated by William H. Willimon.

> [He speaks of] the woeful lack of lay involvement and leadership in most of our worship. Oftentimes Free Church Protestants, who speak the most about "the priesthood of all believers," are the most guilty of promoting clergy-dominated worship in which the minister does all the preaching, praying, speaking, acting, and leading, and the people do all the passive sitting and listening. We can do more on Sunday morning to lift up the ministry of *all* Christians in our worship, not just the ministry of the ordained Christians.[3]

Responsive readings, creeds, and litanies are not new ideas to involve people in worship, but they have fallen into disuse—especially in the evangelical community. Sometimes when a function degenerates to ineffectiveness because of overuse or abuse we assume it is the vehicle which is weak. By not using the vehicles of responsive readings, creeds, and litanies, we *all* are the real losers, for we all suffer from a lack of participation.

READING RESPONSIVELY

Responsive readings are as old as the Torah. But here again, we tend to participate poorly. Our hymnals are often of limited help. Usually there seems to be little thought given to the presentation of responsive readings in a hymnal; there is just a mechanical interchange of dark type and light in alternating verses. Some of the newer hymnals are showing more sensitivity to this issue, for which we are glad.

Biblical examples of responsive readings suggest a sensitivity to subject matter, a thoughtful use of dramatic symbolism, and a genuine interplay by leaders and members of the congregation (sometimes with more than one group).

We may think of the dramatic reading of the cursings and blessings of the Mosaic covenant as ratified by the people in the land of Canaan under the leadership of Joshua. Moses was instructed by the Lord to have his successor lead the people in a truly memorable confrontation with the words of the covenant. Six tribes were to stand upon Mount Gerizim to read words of God's blessing to the people, and six tribes were to stand upon Mount Ebal to read words of cursing to the people should they not obey Yahweh. The topography of the region of Shechem is such that Mount Gerizim is lush and green, but Mount Ebal is usually barren and brown. The curses were to be read from the mountain that suggests a lack of blessing by its very appearance. The blessings were to be recited from the mountain that pictured the hand of the Lord. In this dramatic fashion (Deuteronomy 27:12-13), the congregation of Israel would bring themselves into an unforgettable experience in the words of the covenant. Here was responsive reading that worked!

READING RESPONSIBLY

One hapless pastor led his congregation in the morning reading by saying, "Let us read responsibly," when he meant to say "responsively." Actually, his mix-up with words suggests a splendid idea. That is exactly how we ought to read, even when we read responsively. Responsive reading of the Psalms, for example, can be improved dramatically by an understanding of Hebrew poetry as it is presented in English translations.[4] Rather than the alternate saying of the verses, as is usually done, the phrases of poetry should be divided among various readers. This will greatly enhance the aesthetic appreciation of the Psalm; this type of reading will also help the Psalm to be understood more readily.

Here is an example from the opening words of Psalm 103.

Leader:	Bless the LORD, O my soul;
Congregation:	And all that is within me, bless His holy name.
Leader:	Bless the LORD, O my soul,
Congregation:	And forget none of His benefits;
Congregation Left:	Who pardons all your iniquities;
Congregation Right:	Who heals all your diseases;
Congregation Left:	Who redeems your life from the pit;
Congregation Right:	Who crowns you with lovingkindness and compassion;
Congregation Left:	Who satisfies your years with good things,
Congregation Right:	So that your youth is renewed like the eagle.

In such a reading the entire congregation has come under the blessing of God by the mutual responses to these beautiful words. Such a format does not take long to prepare and could easily be placed inside the bulletin as an insert.

Here is another example from the opening words of the Sermon on the Mount, the Beatitudes (Matthew 5:1-12).

Leader:	And when He saw the multitudes, He went up on the mountain; and after He sat down, His disciples came to Him. And opening His mouth He began to teach them, saying,
Choir:	Blessed are the poor in spirit,
Congregation:	for theirs is the kingdom of heaven.
Choir:	Blessed are those who mourn,
Congregation:	for they shall be comforted.
Choir:	Blessed are the gentle,
Congregation:	for they shall inherit the earth.
Choir:	Blessed are those who hunger and thirst for righteousness,
Congregation:	for they shall be satisfied.
Choir:	Blessed are the merciful,

Congregation:	for they shall receive mercy.
Choir:	Blessed are the pure in heart,
Congregation:	for they shall see God.
Choir:	Blessed are the peacemakers,
Congregation:	for they shall be called sons of God.
Choir:	Blessed are those who have been persecuted for the sake of righteousness,
Congregation:	for theirs is the kingdom of heaven.
Leader:	Blessed are you when men cast insults at you, and persecute you, and say all kinds of evil against you falsely, on account of Me. Rejoice, and be glad, for your reward in heaven is great, for so they persecuted the prophets who were before you.

Here truly is an opportunity for the congregation to bless each other as each member says and hears in a new way, "beautiful words, wonderful words, wonderful words of Life."

CREDO

The principal words we wish to read in a worship service are the words of the Scriptures. But there are two other types of words formally spoken we might also use which may greatly enhance our worship of God in the community. These are the *creed* and the *litany*.

Churches, like individuals, tend to fluctuate between extremes. Certainly this is the case with the use and non-use of creeds. In some congregations where the Gospel as we understand it is rarely preached and the truths of the Scripture seem to be scarcely believed, the tradition of reciting creeds continues. Pastor and congregation in a "Protestant rosary" say great words with seemingly little meaning.

And what about those churches where the Gospel is proclaimed and the truth of Scripture is taught? In these churches it is uncommon to find the confession of the ancient creeds of the Church. What a paradox!

One could come to an erroneous conclusion respecting saying and believing, given these observations. It might seem that those who say they believe do not, and that those who do not say, do. We would be wrong on both counts. Undoubtedly there are many congregants who truly believe the words of the creeds they recite; conversely, in those churches where the creeds are not said, there are surely those who do not believe them! Slander becomes too easy a matter when we look at different traditions.

Again we are back at the issue of *art and heart*. The art of saying a creed is valid only when the creed proceeds from the heart. But for those of us who have the truth in our heart, the art should really follow. "Let the redeemed of the Lord say so"; and let them say so together. In the context of faith, the "pattern of sound words" serves to reinforce, to remind, to direct rightly. In a context of unbelief, all the words of the great creeds of the Church become another "noisy gong" or "clanging cymbal."

Despite a long-held Baptist tradition, "no creed but Christ," the congregational recitation of a creed of the faith is a good act of corporate worship. The danger in a creed is one of reductionism; a possible conclusion that the creed has said all of the truth. But such could really be said of any statement of faith.

THE BIBLE AND CREEDS

Precedents for creeds are not lacking in the Bible. In the Old Testament, the words of Deuteronomy 6:4-9 (along with 11:18-23) had a creedal force. By the words of the great *shema'*, the congregation of Israel confessed her faith in the living God:

> *Hear, O Israel!*
> *Yahweh, our God!*
> *Yahweh alone!*
>
> (Deuteronomy 6:4, our translation)

In the New Testament we find several portions that are suggestive of creedal formulations. Paul's words to Timothy may speak not only of individual confession of faith, but of corporate creedal confession as well.

> *Fight the good fight of faith;*
> *take hold of the eternal life*
>   *to which you were called,*
> *and you made the good confession*
>   *in the presence of many witnesses.*
>
> (1 Timothy 6:12)

Some regard the words of Philippians 2:6-11 and Colossians 1:15-20 to be early creedal formulations. Whether sung as hymns or recited as confessions, these words suggest the public statement of faith. Similarly, the words of 1 Timothy 3:16 present an overlapping of hymn and creed.

> *Beyond all question, the mystery of godliness is great:*
>
> *He appeared in a body,*
>   *was vindicated by the Spirit,*
> *was seen by angels,*
>   *was preached among the nations,*
> *was believed on in the world,*
>   *was taken up in glory.*[5]   (NIV)

We do not suggest that the New Testament presents a full-scale creed in the technical sense, but it certainly points to a common belief structure, to "a web of saving truth."[6] We who believe in truth in God should *confess* it before each other and in the presence of God. By these words we may practice our words of faith and so order our lives. Our words of public confession may also be "beautiful words, wonderful words, wonderful words of Life."

TOGETHER, LET US SPEAK

The second type of word presentations that we may use in the community of the faithful is the *litany*.

A litany is a form of prayer (usually addressed directly to God) in which a leader and the congregation take part alternately with recitations and fixed responses. With some preparation and prayerful forethought, we can place into our people's hands (and into their mouths) some tasteful and meaningful words which can be expressed in unison. Ultimately the words are directed to the hearts of all gathered. These can, and should, be written for specific occasions and situations with specific church bodies in mind. While some can be found printed in various sources, it is best simply to use these as models and write your own.

One of the most beautiful illustrations of the litany is in Psalm 136. The refrain *"His lovingkindness is everlasting"* is repeated twenty-six times; the phrase concludes *every* verse. Perhaps this repetition could seem to be redundant, but if so it is not the fault of the truth being emphasized. And what a truth to be emphasized! When any truth of this significance becomes redundant it is the fault of the insensitive, unreceptive heart of the worshiper. When a phrase like this is repeated, it should gain intensity and excitement as the truth consumes and motivates us. The same phrase is used in Psalm 118, probably in an antiphonal manner.

> *Give thanks to Yahweh, for He is good;*
> *For His lovingkindness is everlasting.*
> *Oh let Israel say,*
> *"His lovingkindness is everlasting."*
> *Oh let the house of Aaron say,*
> *"His lovingkindness is everlasting."*
> *Oh let those who fear the* LORD *say,*
> *"His lovingkindness is everlasting."*   (Verses 1-4)

Look at the litany of blessing in Psalm 103:20-22.

> *Praise Yahweh, you his angels,*
> *you mighty ones who do his bidding,*
> *who obey his word.*
> *Praise Yahweh, all his heavenly hosts,*
> *you his servants who do his will.*
> *Praise Yahweh, all his works*
> *everywhere in his dominion.*
> *Praise Yahweh, O my soul.*   (NIV)

In Psalms 124 and 129 we find the words *"Let Israel now say."* This would indicate that the people were being led in a corporate response with regard to the great and mighty works God was doing and had done in their midst. God's people in all ages ought to praise Him verbally, rejoicing in the wonders of His glorious work. The litany style is one good way to accomplish this.

Congregational response can be experienced by writing your own litanies for significant occasions. Examples are: the commissioning or ordination of pastors or missionaries, the dedication of a building or an instrument, the observances of a special season or day of emphasis (like church education, or missions). The format is to present carefully worded, significant statements with which sincere hearts can agree, followed by a brief sentence for the congregation to express their agreement (just as in Psalm 136—*"His lovingkindness is everlasting"*).

The following are only examples. Please use them that way; not because they could not be copied but because for your situation you must think and pray your way through the best way to say it! Your situation is unique and deserving of this special effort.

MISSIONARY COMMISSIONING

Leader:	To the ministry of missions with the Auca tribe of Ecuador—
People:	We dedicate these, Your servants.
Leader:	To the end that they may be truly effective in their ministry in life and word—
People:	We dedicate these, Your servants.
Leader:	To the end that the church at home may rejoice in upholding them in prayer and financial support—
People:	We dedicate these, Your servants.
Leader:	To the end that those left at home will rejoice with those who go in all that is accomplished—
People:	We dedicate these, Your servants.
Leader:	To the end that believers in other cultures will

	learn to know the joy and responsibility of carrying out the work of ministry—
People:	We dedicate these, Your servants.
Leader:	To the end that the Lord Jesus Christ, whose great commission these have purposed to help carry out, may receive all the glory due His name—
People:	We dedicate these, Your servants.

ORGAN DEDICATION

Leader:	To the end that God will be glorified, His people will be edified, and that His truth shall be spread throughout the earth—
People:	We humbly dedicate this organ.
Leader:	To the end that those gathered in this place to praise and adore our Lord may be one in desire, one in purpose, and one in harmony—
People:	We prayerfully consecrate this organ.
Leader:	With the desire that those who play, those who hear, and those who sing to the music of this instrument may be drawn closer to our Lord—
People:	We earnestly dedicate this organ.
Leader:	With godly appreciation to those who sacrificially gave to bring this fine instrument to our church—
People:	We thankfully dedicate this organ.
Leader:	With this prayer: O Lord, we corporately place this instrument into your hands to be used only and always for Your glory in all the services of this local body of Christ.
People:	Amen.

FOR THE DEDICATION OF A NEW CHURCH BUILDING

Here is a litany that was written for the dedication of a new church building for the First Baptist Church in Jackson, Minnesota (July 26, 1981).

Leader: To the glory of God the Father; to the honor of God the Son; and to the ministry of God the Holy Spirit.

People: We do now with joy and gratitude dedicate this building.

Leader: God has graciously led us, prospering the work of our hands and granting us the desires of our hearts to bring us this day and to this happy occasion.

People: Because of His faithfulness and goodness, we are gathered in His presence to dedicate this building to its proper and sacred uses, and to the praise and honor of His Holy Name.

Leader: Here, we will gather regularly as instructed in God's Word, for worship, prayer, instruction, and fellowship. Here, we will bring our offerings and gifts for the work of the Lord.

People: Since this new church will encourage us to be actively engaged in these biblical directives, we thank God for it and happily dedicate it to the Lord this day.

Leader: As a congregation we are committed to the infallibility of the Word of God, to the finished work of Christ on the cross for man's personal salvation, to wholesome Christian living by the power of God's Holy Spirit, and to the soon return of our Savior Jesus Christ for all who believe.

People: To these great truths we rededicate ourselves, realizing that not in this new building does God dwell, but in us, for as the Scripture says, we are His house.

Leader: With deep appreciation for all who have had a

part in the ministry of this church in the
past, and with a special prayer for those
who will serve, minister, and fellowship in
this church in the future.

People: We humbly and gratefully dedicate this
building. *To God be the glory, great things
He has done.*

COMMENCEMENT LITANY

Leader: Lord, how may I most effectively demonstrate my years of training for You?

Graduates: I will love the Lord my God with all my
heart, and with all my soul, and with all
my mind, and with all my strength, and I
will do my best to present myself as one
approved, a workman who does not need
to be ashamed and who correctly handles
the Word of truth.

Leader: Lord, how may we well support our
graduates?

Faculty: We will pray "that your love may abound
more and more in knowledge and depth
to insight, so that you may be able to dis-
cern what is best and may be pure and
blameless until the day of Christ, filled
with the fruit of righteousness that
comes through Jesus Christ—to the
glory and praise of God."

Leader: Lord, how may spouses, parents, and
friends support these, Your servants?

Congregation: During these days of preparation, we have
stood beside you, supported you, and
prayed for you. Now, at the milestone of
commencement, we pledge to undergird
your ministry with ever-growing intensity, and extend to you our heartfelt

                         "Congratulations."

Graduates: Now we thank God on your account for your faithfulness to us, and may God grant to us all an ever-increasing awareness of His Glory!

Once you have begun to pray over and think through the ministry of litanies and the way they can give the church member a means of expressing himself in the body, we believe they will find their way into your worship life. The basic rule to follow is to make all these activities relevant to God and His people, and to remember that there are *very few* such elements of a service that should be a weekly occurrence! These, too, are "beautiful words, wonderful words, wonderful words of Life." By our words, said aloud and together, we glorify our great God.

Chapter 12, Notes

[1]The words "translating to give the sense" (Nehemiah 8:8) suggest the possibility that the Hebrew words of the Torah were translated into Aramaic and paraphrased so that the people could understand clearly the words of God through Moses, His prophet. We likely have here both the beginnings of the process that led to the Targumim (Aramaic paraphrases of the Old Testament), as well as a biblical precedent for modern paraphrases of the Bible. Such was the mutual conclusion Ron had one time in a conference call with Dr. William F. Kerr and Dr. Kenneth Taylor, the paraphraser of the enormously successful *Living Bible*.

[2]It is thought by some that the letter from Laodicea is Paul's Epistle to the Ephesians, or perhaps his letter to Philemon.

[3]William H. Willimon, *Word, Water, Wine and Bread: How Worship Has Changed Over the Years* (Valley Forge: Judson Press, 1980), pp. 123-124.

[4]For a presentation of the basic idea of Hebrew poetry, see Ronald Barclay Allen, *Praise! A Matter of Life and Breath* (Nashville: Thomas Nelson, 1980), chapter 4.

[5]Ralph P. Martin writes: "The hymn of 1 Timothy iii, 16 is a clear instance of an early confession of faith by which the Church gave expression to the fundamental facts and truths of the Gospel. The first words which are quoted above tell us this explicitly: 'Great indeed, *we confess* . . .' [A. V.], At this point hymns and creeds meet and overlap." *Worship in the Early Church* (Grand Rapids: Eerdmans, 1974), p. 53.

[6]Ibid., p. 55. Martin refers to the following passages which use phrases that speak of a "web of saving truth": Acts 2:42 ("The apostles' teaching"); Philippians 2:16 ("The word of life"); Romans 6:17 ("The standard of teaching"—RSV); 1 Timothy 4:6 ("The words of faith and good doctrine"); 2 Timothy 1:13 ("The pattern of sound words"); and 2 Timothy 4:3 ("Sound teaching;" also in Titus 1:9).

Chapter 13

The Gift of Song

"This Our Song of Grateful Praise"

*A*gain and again in Scripture we are commanded and admonished to sing to the Lord. Singing for those redeemed by the grace of God should not be an obligation; rather, it is a freely given expression. It seems to us totally inconsistent to be a joyful believer and a non-singer! When a non-singer becomes a Christian, he or she becomes a singer. Not all are blessed with a finely tuned ear and a well modulated voice; so the sound may not be superb—it may even be out-of-tune and off-key. Remember: worship and service are a state of heart; musical sound is a state of art. Let's not make the mistake of confusing them.

THERE ARE STANDARDS

As a choral conductor for nearly three decades, Gordon has been an active part of some very exciting music making. Any credible director must work for the best results he feels his ensemble is capable of producing. These involve:

1. Blend, the ability to match vowels;
2. Intonation, the ability to tune well;
3. Tone color, the free, unforced singing voice;
4. Rhythmic integrity, singing to the point of the beat;

5. A sense of music, interpretation suitable to the period and style of the music.

However, with the exception of passages which deal with excellence in more general terms, one searches the Scripture in vain for authority on how to sing. We do not find Scripture to support a vocal/choral/instrumental technique or pedagogy!

Scripture does not tell us how to sing, as far as the art is concerned; but it does tell us how to sing as far as the heart is concerned. We are to "sing with the spirit and with the mind also" (1 Corinthians 14:15). To a musician, music has a great spirit of its own. Singing with the spirit of the New Testament sense is singing in concert with the Holy Spirit whose task is focusing on Christ. The deliberate purpose of Christian singing is to exert all the dynamic of this powerful expression to glorify God. Notice the passage goes on to say not only with spirit but also with the mind. How very important it is to *think* praise as well as verbalize it.

WHEN GROUPS SING

Gordon frequently leads large groups, composed mostly of believers, in corporate singing. Here are some of the more obvious scenes that occur. Some sing with boundless joy and a glow on their faces which seem clearly to say "I love the Lord, and I want Him (and everybody else) to know it." Others may not even open the hymnal; they just exist until we get to something they feel is important. These people seem to have no sense of joy, no concert with the Spirit in praise. Still other singers in the groups may go through the motions, open their books and their mouths in seeming dynamic participation. If, however, you were to ask one of them to paraphrase even one thought from the hymn when it was over— they would be at a loss for words. The words had gone in the eyes and out the mouth but never penetrated the mind and heart. And then there are those who occasionally, while busily singing spiritually stimulating truth, nod a friendly hello to a latecomer strolling down the aisle. If concentration were directed on the thought of the hymn there would scarcely be consciousness of another's presence.

Some sing only if they "know" the song; if the title is unfamiliar, the book may just remain in the rack. They do not want to have to think, to read and grasp something unfamiliar. All too often, the familiar is sung thoughtlessly while the unknown remains unknown.

The best way for believers to sing the praise of God is to simply *do that!* We are not to wait for a good tune (whether that means old or new), not to wait until "I feel like it," not to wait until everyone else is singing so lustily that no one would hear us. We are admonished to sing to the Lord, not to the next pew. Singing so our brothers and sisters in Christ can hear us can be encouraging to them. Surely the Church does not lack for spiritual, spirited music to sing; but all too often it lacks spirit motivated, spiritual singers to join in the song.

AN INSTRUCTION TOWARD BALANCE

Colossians 3:16 and Ephesians 5:19 present instruction on singing, telling us to balance our singing. These verses are probably not referring to specific kinds of songs when they say psalms, hymns, and spiritual songs, but the idea of balance seems indicated.

1. *Psalms*. These are obviously selections from the hymnbook of Israel. There seems to be a healthy revival of psalm singing today. At some points in Church history (and in some communions even today) psalms were the exclusive diet.[1]

2. *Hymns*. Not as easily defined, but would seem to be those songs about God (His attributes, etc.) and addressed to God.

3. *Spiritual songs*. They were probably referring to an improvised song made up from the heart in spontaneous praise. Do you sing to the Lord in your devotional life? Make up some songs from your heart; they need not be written down—they are for the moment. "Spiritual songs" could also be applied to the concept of songs of our experience and testimony addressed to one another.

By whatever means one chooses to identify psalms, hymns, and spiritual songs, it seems clear there is to be a variety of expression. All expressions balanced give us our musical language for worship. The art is superceded by the heart which is to be filled with thanksgiving. God is interested in the thankful heart, the involved spirit, and the active mental participation of the singers of His song. The refinement of the art naturally follows the dedicated heart in singing to the Lord.

But even this refinement is not necessary—especially in cases where a dedicated heart is not capable of refinement. The story is told of a leper isolated in a colony held captive by disease and society. Though few on earth cared, the gospel of Christ had reached the heart of the poor outcast through the ministry of missions. God had put a song in her heart (as He has in *all* His redeemed), but the disease had progressed and the vocal mechanism had been largely eaten away. Film footage shows her clutching a few pages from the hymnal, trying to sing to the Lord. What sound there was did not even resemble music, but God looks at the *heart*. It just may have been some of the most beautiful music ever heard in heaven; one of the redeemed singing with spirit and understanding, and thanksgiving unto the Lord.

MUSIC IS POWERFUL

It would be difficult to overstate the power of the musical language. It has emotional-mental stimulation unmatched by any other means of communication. Words alone can be and often are very strong, but couple them with the "right" music and they can be burned into the mind and consciousness indelibly.

God gave us this gift of music that we might develop it and use it to express our creativity in praise and worship. Psalm 92:1-3 reads,

> *It is good to praise Yahweh*
> *and make music to your name, O Most High,*
> *to proclaim your love in the morning*
> *and your faithfulness at night,*

> to the music of the ten-stringed lyre
> and the melody of the harp.   (NIV)

It is beyond our purpose here to delve deeply into the natural laws of physics as regards tonality, but it is clear that the Lord placed the ability to generate and respond to music within the human race. Early in Scripture we read, *"Then Moses and the sons of Israel sang this song to the LORD, and said, 'I will sing to the LORD, for He is highly exalted; . . .' "* (Exodus 15:1). Each time God did great things for His people they burst into songs of praise.

To sing when one is happy and full of joy is a most natural expression. God has placed in us a happy song when all is going well. Consider the whistle of the man busily involved in satisfying occupation (it is most unusual to hear one whistle who is despondent or for whom life has lost purpose). Or think of the song of the wife busily cleaning the kitchen or on her way to work reflecting over the joy of living.

There are two reasons for the lack of songs among people in our present society:

1. The pressure of life without purpose (without Christ) in our hectic, explosive world takes the song right out of a person;

2. The fact that we are surrounded with music in the home, car, business, doctor's office, restaurant, etc., makes it unnecessary to sing ourselves. We need silence filled with an awareness of God and all He has done in Christ Jesus—before long you will fill your silence with *your song!* In the words of an excellent piece, "God gave the song"!

God does know the power of song for the believer. And He recorded several instances of song and singing in the Bible. Some include:

1. The morning stars singing together (Job 38:7).

2. The song of deliverance from the Egyptians (Exodus 15:1-21).

3. The songs of praise throughout the Psalms.

4. The antiphonal song of the two choirs at the worship of dedicating the rebuilt walls (Nehemiah 12:40).

5. The new song of the redeemed in Christ (Colossians 3:16).

6. The song of the redeemed and the angels gathered around the throne in Revelation (Revelation 5:9-10; 12, 13). From the beginning to the end of the sacred canon the power of musical expression is evident![2]

SATAN AND THE WORLD KNOW MUSIC'S POWER

The prince of the power of the air has full knowledge of the power of music. Have you noticed how he frequently takes good things God has made for us to enjoy and develop, then perverts and pollutes them for his purposes and does great damage to both the art and to the heart? Satan has gripped and influenced our present generation to sin, compromise, lust, deceit, etc., and one of his most effective "tools" has been music. God made it to praise Himself. Satan has used and abused it to detract and frustrate the praise of God. An idea (either good or bad) set to a good melody, given rhythmic intensity and harmonic consistency, can really work its way into our minds. Science tells us we are what we eat; the Bible tells us we are what we think. The devil has made such use of music that one could almost come to the conclusion that it is the music which is evil. The fact is, that it is the heart which is deceived and the mind polluted. The devil simply knows what God has always known, that music is a powerful way to get his ideas implanted and affect the behavior of mankind.

Want to sell your product? Whether Chevrolets, Pepsi, chewing gum, bathroom tissue, or mouthwash, sellers know to sell it you must sing it! Compose a catchy tune, present it in a clever way, and the product becomes known. Millions of dollars are spent each year to write and record these sales jingles. In the pragmatic world of business you can be sure they would not do it if it did not pay. Music can extol the virtue of the product, tell you many reasons why your life is not complete until you buy it, and keep you coming back for more after you have "experienced" it. That is exactly why God gave music to His people; to extol His worth, to know Him, and to retain fresh fellowship with Him.

WHEN WILL THE CHURCH LEARN ITS POWER?

Music, God's idea of a marvelous expression for His people, has been prostituted by Satan, made merchandise by business, and generally ignored by the Church. While there are some notable exceptions to the above statement, it must be conceded to be generally true. There are some artists of real integrity who, while not knowing God in Christ in the biblical sense, have done real service to the musical art. There are some businesses which retain integrity to the art. And there are some churches which have realized the vast potential of the musical ministry.

There are, however, many scores of churches ignoring music or snubbing it as a frill. Some are even convinced it is a potential source of friction that is better left alone. Some see it as a necessary evil which the "musical among us" seem to need. Of course, many feel it is a good time filler, a part of the preliminaries until we get down to the important parts of the service. Some see it for what it really is or surely should be.

MUSIC IS..

1. . . . one of the church's very best means of extolling God for who He is and what He has done. It may be a perfect corporate or individual expression. It allows any and all of the people to say something of real importance to and about God.

2. . . . one of the very best ways to teach biblical truth. God's word, both directly and conceptually set to music, can penetrate the mind and heart and stay there. What we sing, we remember, because we have combined the power of intellect with emotion.

3. . . . one of the very best ways to spread the message of the Gospel to an unbelieving society. While we cannot find "music in evangelism" specifically mentioned in the Bible, it has proven to be effective in outreach. Throughout the history of evangelism and missions, music can be found to play an important role. Great strides are being made in the task of

making music tastefully relevant to those to be reached both in a culture or sub-culture, and cross-culturally. Learning continues as men and women make honest efforts in these areas of music outreach.

Churches Are Awakening

Throughout our country more and more local congregations are seeing the need for musical leadership and guidance in their church. The priority of seeking good lay leadership or college/seminary trained ministers of music comes sometimes immediately after the pastoral position is properly filled. A person who is willing, sensitive to the Holy Spirit with good "hands on" experience in music leadership, and who is more committed to ministry than to music is ideal. If his or her highest calling is to God and he or she has leadership/musical capabilities, this one's concept of God and the ministry will propel him or her to excellence in the art of the craft. All God wants of His servants is everything they have and are. This calling is the constant challenge to demonstrate a high regard for God and His people which will give rise to the finest artistic development of which one is capable.

One of the foremost objectives in any local assembly is to develop the congregational choir. While conducting styles vary, the spiritual-musical leadership of the entire gathered body can give significant direction to an entire meeting. Music must be selected for its relevance to the service theme. If there is no theme, at least the musical portion can have one. Think toward variety (of key, tempo, style, etc.), but also have a sense of unity.

Encourage the participants to get involved totally, yet on a spiritual level. Remarks like "Let's raise the roof," or "Sing so they can hear us two blocks away," or "Look happy while you sing," should be avoided. We sing to express ourselves to God and to one another. Direct the people into the text. If it is not worthy, we should not sing it; if it is worthy, we are to sing with understanding. Direct toward singing for the joy of holy expression, the sheer thrill of redemption. Occasionally we must draw special attention to a stanza or phrase; if deep meaning is pointed out, people are more prone to begin watching for themselves.

On occasion, if the mood of the meeting allows for it, it is good to rehearse the congregation. Select a strong hymn or gospel song which may be less known to the people. Research it, know how it came to be written, and discover how it relates to us today and to this occasion. Now have it played or sung so the people begin to get the idea. Have everyone sing a stanza on the melody, then for the sake of those who cannot reach it, introduce parts. It *is possible* for congregations to sing in harmony—this is a beautiful symbol of our consonant relationship. If the organist can play all parts while the pianist plays the alto line in octaves, everyone should then sing alto. Now join together again, encouraging congregants to sing where they fit best. This can be done on all parts if audience attention is holding. Gordon has spent as much as twenty minutes with a congregation doing this, and by the end, it not only sounds beautiful but the people have had a most meaningful spiritual and musical experience.

Once the congregation begins to grasp the beauty of musical ministry, other choirs and ensembles, both vocal and instrumental, are a natural outgrowth. It is beyond the scope of this discussion to develop the entire music program; there are many fine books on that subject. Know that if there is to be real ministry in music, it will begin in the heart of the people; the art will follow as meaningful leadership is developed.

The people of God have always been and will always be a people of song. If the enjoyment of song is gone, that is a symptom of far greater disease. A congregation's singing is not an absolute thermometer of their spiritual temperature, but it is one indicator. As Luther said way back in the Reformation days of the 16th century, "If any would not sing and talk of what Christ has wrought for us, he shows thereby that he does not really believe . . ."[3]

SOME OBSERVATIONS ON MUSICAL STYLE

Throughout the modern history of the Church, music has been a subject of substantial controversy. Sometimes it even becomes militant! Before we say too much here, remember that it is always Satan's plan to keep God's people off balance, and out of focus. If he can get us to argue and bicker over something—*anything* that can keep us from concentrating on bringing glory to God—he will do it. Down through the years, music has been one area he has selected to drive wedges between God's people. Why? Because music is such an effective, powerful means of expression. If Satan can keep us arguing about it, while we are not looking, he will use one of our best offensive weapons against us! It is such a subjective area that tastes come into play very strongly.

Sometimes we even try to build moral/theological fences to defend our taste. Once again, we are dealing with a heart/art matter. If we concentrate too hard on defending our point of view with regard to art, our heart may slip into vile hypocrisy. Satan has never been concerned over which side of the boat God's people fall out. As a defeated enemy he will go to any extreme to disarm our effectiveness and, regrettably, he is too often successful.

As far back as Pope Gregory, the Roman Catholic Church tried to "canonize" music. There are still orders of the Church which wholeheartedly subscribe to the Gregorian chant. It is very beautiful, and the art form is well established and generally intact. Time has passed and the mainstream of the Roman church has left it behind. Other attempts have been made to canonize music. Some strong leader or movement comes to the conclusion that they have "found it" and established the musical style to be used henceforth. While some have agreed to stop right there (splinter groups can be found of nearly all extreme positions), there have always been those who go on. History indicates that the body which canonizes musical form and style begins to "fossilize" right there. The very nature of music which has brought the church much good, demands that it will continue to develop and change. Sometimes we wish it would stop, but it will not.

Some of the prominent theologians of yesteryear held some very strong opinions about music. Usually these were very narrow, intolerant positions; most of them would make us smile today. John Calvin insisted that "only God's word is worthy to be sung in God's praise"; hymns of human composition were forbidden. The first book published on our shores was the *Bay Psalm Book,* and early Christian settlers sang primarily psalms until the mid-eighteenth century. Luther borrowed tunes from the secular arena in his day and for that received much criticism. Pietists of the mid-eighteenth century generally rejected art music and set out to create a more pure "church music."

WHAT WILL IT BE?

The musical ball bounces back and forth between traditional and experimental or popular. During periods of spiritual renewal the traditional is frequently set to one side and more popular expression sets in. Too often much which has great value is thrown out in favor of the fresh and unproven. We must learn to balance valid contemporary expression with that which is worthy from the past. Both are needed and significant!

There has been endless debate, to the point of the ridiculous, over all the basics of music: Is it appropriate and fitting for Christian music? The overriding concern should be one of intent. If the heart of the composer/performer of musical expression is set on God and bringing Him praise and honor, then he will be bound to offer a sacrifice of integrity. He will seek a text which is biblically sound and set it to music which helps communicate that text in an artistic, relevant way. And we can evaluate those words in the light of biblical truth. In Christian expression the music must always be the servant of the text—it must help make it meaningful and communicative.

Questions—and eyebrows—have been raised when discussing the areas of harmony and rhythm in musical compositions both today and in years past. At one time in Church music history the melodic intervals were questioned; certain skips were considered sensual. Harmonic intervals had to be approved. It was permissible to sing in unison, 4ths or 5ths; but 3rds and 6ths were deemed sensual and forbidden. Today harmony is more apt to be seen for what it is: a musical device to be used at the creative discretion of the composer to say what is called for textually and contextually.

When Sir Arthur Sullivan wrote *Onward Christian Soldiers*

for the parish children to sing as they marched to a children's rally in a neighboring town, many of the established parishioners frowned on its militant, "unsolemn" rhythm. Now it appears in most hymnals. The composer never dreamed it would be a standard one day, nor that the conservative Salvation Army would have a vital theme song!

The waltz rhythm made so famous a century ago by Johann Strauss was a real shock to some in the audiences of the Moody-Sankey meetings. Ira Sankey, the inspiring song leader for Dwight L. Moody, used some contemporary music to relate to the unbelievers who would be more familiar with the waltz sound. The established church folks had much negative reaction, yet for years we have had waltzes in our hymnals. They were once the latest; now they are slightly ho-hum in a meeting of youth.

And so it goes, music continually in a state of flux. Who among us would not like to see it stay as it was in the "good old days"? But, as Ken Medema has expressed it, "You can't go back to the music of yesterday!" At least, not all of us can go back, and not all of the time. Remember, the question is not one of art, but attitude; and for the believer, it is God who must be on the heart's throne!

MUSIC AND "OTHER" CULTURES

There has long been a tendency to impose our taste and culture upon others we may be trying to affect with the Gospel. With written and spoken language it is common practice to learn the native tongue and dialect so communication becomes possible. More recently it has become a priority for missionaries to learn the culture in order to avoid social errors which could severely curtail meaningful encounter with the nationals. No thoughtful missionary would go to a people of unknown tongue and differing culture and continue to speak his own language saying, "I have great, good news for you. You keep listening to me talk and eventually you'll figure out what I'm saying, then you, too, will know the good news." Of course not! Marvelous work is done in the area of language study to make it possible not only to speak a given language, but also to write it so that the Word of God is available in a clearly understandable context.

Musically we have not progressed that far. Only recently has there been a serious effort to help churches established in other cultures compose and sing their very own expression reflecting native tonality, rhythms, and other distinguishing factors. Current studies and efforts in ethnomusicology and ethnohymnology reveal significant steps which, while overdue, are most encouraging.

Within our own culture there are numerous subcultures. Sometimes we go into one of these with music which is above or below or to one side or the other from where our prospective audience may be. Our hymnals are filled with much important and relevant music for our churches and surely this is no call for their overthrow. But our hymnals are composed largely of common and triple meter rhythms and melodies of past generations as in a march or waltz, with block harmonies and predictable rhythms. The youth culture is not there. We must be sensitive to what they will hear as we attempt to reach them. Once reached, they can and should be introduced to their rich Christian heritage, and we should encourage a marriage of contemporary and traditional expression which has artistic integrity.

Exactly the same music could be a stepping stone or a stumbling block. Music really used by the Holy Spirit to reach a person outside one's particular cultural/musical framework may be downright shocking to the uninitiated. For generations folks have known what they have liked and liked what they have known. Outside the familiar circle, whether one swings to the traditional/classical side or to the contemporary/avant-garde side, some will feel most uncomfortable. New pieces are sometimes accepted as long as they remain within the known boundaries of tonality and rhythm, but let them sound strange and the reaction is assured. May we have openness to grow in our circle of the familiar so that our eyes are on ministry and intent and not on whether we recognize the specific art form. It is a musician's responsibility to know his audience and be sensitive to appropriateness.

One whose heart is set on ministry is not going to try to shock the uninitiated. Sensitive artists are more interested in building bridges than walls—we want to communicate! May both hearers and performers in music ministry be sensitive to the power of God tastefully realized through the power of music.

CODA

We have attempted a very broad discussion here. Entire books have been written on nearly every issue and idea mentioned.[4] Our purpose has been to bring church music expression into perspective with our "state of heart" concept. Too often other issues eclipse this all important one. We miss the boat when we enter long discussions on style, on whether the modern sound is permitted or whether we should insist upon a steady musical diet of the "established" hymns and anthems. The fact is *any* music done in the name of ministry which places art over heart is not pleasing to God. It could be the most glorious performance of Brahms "Requiem," which we dearly love, or a very well rehearsed and presented "now sound." God knows the intent; His questions are for the heart. If the heart is right, there will be a holy demand for artistic integrity far above the standard set if art were on the throne!

May God help us to recognize music as God's gift to express ourselves to Him and to one another. May the Holy Spirit of God quicken our hearts to develop and cherish this gift with all artistic integrity. May God grant that music and musicians who know Christ will place all their energies into the ministry of praising God; building up His people and reaching the unbelieving community with the clear, unclouded Gospel of Christ.

Chapter 13, Notes

[1]Grady Hardin speaks of the use of the psalms in Christian worship. He says: "There are encouraging signs of a renewed interest in the psalms. Some ministers and music leaders are 'lining out' psalms very much like were sung in early American churches when books were rare and literacy was limited. The quality of praise is increased when a line of a psalm is sung to a free and simple tune by the leader and then repeated by the congregation. The simple tune is not a problem and the words which the people repeat carry the meaning." *The Leadership of Worship* (Nashville: Abingdon, 1980), p. 38.

We may also cite the continuing use of the psalms by many Reformed communions as their sole worship music. One Reformed communion has recently published a Psalter based strictly on Genevan tunes.

Further, as a contrasting use of the psalms in Christian worship, we may mention the vastly popular Praise albums published by Maranatha! Music. Many of the worship choruses in these albums are from the psalms.

[2]Chuck Fromm has presented a more expansive listing of the use of music in the Bible and in various periods in the Church. See his *Back to Basics: A Study of Public Music Ministry* (Costa Mesa: Ministry Resource Center, 1981).

[3]Walter E. Buszin, *Luther on Music*, p. 6, from the Foreword of the Babst *Gesangbuch* of 1945, cited by Donald P. Hustad, *Jubilate: Church Music in the Evangelical Tradition* (Carol Stream, Ill.: Hope, 1981), p. 243.

[4]See the bibliography at the end of this book.

Chapter 14

An Environment for Worship

*"Sing Them Over Again to Me—
Let Me More of Their Beauty See!"*

*I*n this chapter we wish to present factors relating to the physical environment for worship. Some readers might sense that the issues of acoustics, building design, color, instruments and their placement, sound systems, lighting, furnishing, and the appearance of worship leaders are rather prosaic for a book which seeks to speak to issues of heart in worship. But the factors we discuss in this chapter concern not just art; they affect heart attitudes as well in a manifold variety of ways. The very subtlety of some of these issues respecting moods of worship is deceiving; these issues are real. They are a matter of appearance *and* heart motive.

Furthermore, these factors are important irrespective of size or location of the worship center. Some homes, for example, are more conducive for worship than others for the small house-church. Some large buildings are only that—big! A (clean) barn might inspire more enthusiastic singing!

That these factors are truly spiritual in intent—and not material only—may be demonstrated by a perusal of the many chapters of the Torah of Moses which speak of many of the same kinds of issues for the building of the Tabernacle. Remember, that was just a tent!

WHAT TO CALL THE MEETING ROOMS

Before we describe elements in the environment for worship, we will discuss what to call the room in which we gather. The term *sanctuary* is often felt to be misleading for a Christian assembly room for worship. For many people, the word sanctuary suggests that there is something special about the building, and that this word detracts from the New Testament reality that the church is the people of God. God's people are His temple; His Spirit resides in the believer (see 1 Corinthians 3:16-17; 6:18-20).

However, when the people of God are gathered in a particular building or room for worship, we find nothing wrong with the term *sanctuary*, as the building—at that moment, at least—is a true *sanctum*, a genuine holy place.

We do object to the word *auditorium*, however, for that word suggests that we come to sit and listen. The gathering place of the people of God is not to be an auditory room only; it is a place for the people to participate.

Some congregations are using the term *worship center* for their assembly building. They have come together not only to hear the Word, but to sing God's praise. Furthermore, they will keep on worshiping God in their private lives, even when not gathered in the community center.

LOST IN THE ACOUSTICS

Have you ever been in a congregation, singing the praise of God in an enthusiastic manner, and yet feeling all alone? If you look around, you may well see that others seem to be singing lustily too, but the sound is lost. In all probability, it is due to a poor acoustical environment. Many of our churches, some of which are quite new, have been built more like a living room or funeral parlor than a meeting place for God's singing saints. These rooms are complete with wall-to-wall carpet and full drapes at the windows and baptistry, acoustically sprayed ceilings, padded pews, and soft-textured walls.

Consider the importance of placing a congregation in an

acoustical environment which invites musical/vocal participation. Since the normal church service time from the beginning of the prelude to the end of the postlude involves activity, half of which is musical, it does not make sense to build a lecture room! Occasionally the assumption is that "a good sound system will fix the problem." More will be said in a few pages about sound systems, but no sound system can remedy a room's poor acoustics.

The most exciting places to sing are rooms with hard walls and floors which resonate and reinforce the sound. Of course, it is possible to overdo the echo in a room to the point of confusion and ear fatigue, but it is easier to take echo out of a room than to put some resonance in!

"We Lost Our Spirit"

An oft-repeated story is told of a church which had experienced rapid growth. Their original building was a very plain, tabernacle-shaped room with synthetic tile floor, plaster walls, and wooden ceiling. With unsafe crowding it was possible to get about 400 enthusiastic congregants into the building. When they sang, one would have thought he was in heaven; with such excitement, the enthusiasm was contagious. The day came when their new building was finally complete. It held 1200 people, had a large carpeted platform and aisles—high, thickly coated ceiling—soft-textured block walls—padded pews and generally very dry acoustics. A few months later the spirit of the congregation had fallen; services were not nearly so exciting. One observed, "It seems the spirit went out of the church when we moved to the new building." In a way he was right. No matter how much prodding a leader might do, the singing never made it. The new room was a large sponge, with virtually no reflective surfaces.

The acoustics must be *bright* enough to give back sound to the congregation. No aspiring pastor desires to lead a *dead* church, yet we who want *live* churches are guilty of killing them acoustically. We have no pat answers which will guarantee a room's success acoustically, except to say keep enough reflective surfaces to keep the room alive. It is much easier to add some carpet, or acoustical panels to absorb too much bounce than to tear out expensive carpet, drapes, and other deadeners.

"WE KEPT OUR SPIRIT"

A congregation across town from the one described above had likewise experienced great growth and needed a new meeting place. They, too, had a chapel which held a few hundred and planned to build a facility seating about 1500. They realized the *live* characteristics of their building greatly enhanced their singing.

Before agreeing to hire an architect, they would take him into the chapel and explain that while they wanted a new building which would please the eye, be appropriately comfortable, and bring real glory to God, it had to sound like the chapel. They went so far as to say, "If the new building doesn't sing like the chapel, you will forfeit your commission." He got the message. Their new building really sings and is also an excellent room for preaching. It is possible to have the best of both. They did use carpet aisle runners and padded pews, but left the platform/choir area hard floor with fairly hard paneled walls and wooden ceiling. When participants learn to walk more lightly, and the choir members do not tap their feet, the hard floor in front makes a wonderful sounding board.

When planning to build and/or remodel, much must be considered. The acoustics have been forgotten all too often and when they have been considered, sometimes the room still turns out too dry. We all prefer to attend and worship in a live church; be sure you do not kill it with acoustical deadness.

SHAPE UP

The shape of a room for worship says much. While we would not necessarily argue for any one preferred shape, the shape does make a statement with regard to the philosophy of ministry if not about a church's very theology. Such factors as the location of the pulpit, communion table, and baptistry all make statements with regard to the priority of the Word and ordinances. Whether or not seating for the congregation is "fixed" (as in installed pews) or flexible (as in folding or stackable chairs) may say something of how the congregation's role is perceived. Generally chairs and pews set in straight rows in the traditional manner are best in the more objective, God-centered environments, and circles or sharply curved rows reflect a more relational, subjective, people-centered ministry.

The best of all situations, it seems, would be the flexibility to set up the worship center according to the particular service planned. This requires great care in planning and maximum custodial help in getting everything arranged. If the Lord's table is being observed, perhaps a circular setting with the table central and the people gathered around it would be effective. When a baptismal service is planned, the axis of the seating would focus toward the baptistry, and this meaningful ordinance would take new significance to both partaker and observer. In events more geared toward preaching, the pulpit would be the focal point and seating could be effectively arranged in rows. For special services of music and pageantry the focus could be any direction determined most effective for the occasion. Aisles could be arranged in the shape of a cross or other meaningful symbol for certain seasons or celebrations. This is one reason that cathedrals through the years have avoided fixed seating since they have so many special services and pageants. Cushions may be made available for times of kneeling.

Somewhat akin to the shape of the room is the height of the ceiling. In an effort to gain maximum floor space for the least building cost, ceilings in many churches have gotten lower. One reason churches have had high ceilings through the years is to draw the eye upward, to give the spirit wings. With the high cost of heating, it is practical to help the cause with physically lower buildings, but the upward look is still desirable. With visual lines, vertical grills, organ pipes, accent colors or panels, the emphasis should draw the eye up, not side to side. Some very creative work is being done in building and remodeling to enhance the upward look.

COLORS AND CHOIRS

Occasionally the colors of the worship center are chosen because the paint is on sale or the custodian feels a certain color would make for easier care. Recent studies indicate that the color of the environment has potent psychological and attention ramifications. Warmer colors (reds, yellows, oranges) tend to create activity, restlessness, nerves more on edge, wakefulness. In the theater the off-stage waiting room is known as the green room (it is literally green), because that color is relaxing without being too calming or anesthetic. Shades of blue are also restful. Police stations are now placing violent people in Baker pink surroundings, finding the color calms maniacs unbelievably, making them manageable, sometimes literally passive. Surroundings with restful colors, neutral colors (beiges), and dark wood paneling are easy environments in which to fall asleep—either literally or mentally. We make no specific statement which would identify the ideal color combination; the purpose here is to make one aware that it is a factor. While the art of color will not generate heart worship, it is a consideration of anyone who takes the worship setting seriously.

The possible locations for choirs and instruments are almost unlimited, but there are some very practical considerations which are overlooked with amazing consistency. The choir must be located in such a manner as to be able to hear one another and hear their accompanying instrument(s). Vocal ensemble is difficult to achieve under good physical and acoustical conditions and virtually impossible in many places. Most church-style organs have remote sound sources (not contained in the console). These must be located near enough to the choir and organist so a proper balance can be heard by the musicians. We have observed a building where the choir seating was in one corner of the front and the organ console and speaker system were in the other. There are approximately fifty feet of space separating the two. If the organist plays loud enough for the choir to hear and remain in tune, he cannot hear the choir; if he softens enough to hear them, they lose their support and begin to fade away—this frustrates all concerned. An extreme example, but indicative of a rather typical lack of planning ahead.

Choir seating should be on risers which have plenty of rise between rows. While seating arrangements can take height into account, there are many other musical considerations. Rows should have a minimum of ten inches graduation; this allows for greater sight and sound line. Also, choirs should be seated in such a way as not to be too wide for their depth. No row should be wider than twenty seats, unless the acoustics are extremely favorable. Standing a little deeper and not quite so wide generally helps develop choral unity.

When both piano and organ are to be placed for use in a worship room, they should be located close to each other (preferably with keyboards side by side). Many churches in the evangelical community place these instruments on each side of a wide platform; this renders it very difficult for musicians to play together sensitively. The music director/song leader also has more difficulty in conducting, since those who should follow him are so spread out, forcing a wide directing attention area. These may seem to be picky things, but they make the difficult task of effective church music even more difficult, especially for relatively less trained church music leadership.

There has been some experimentation with seating the choir in the congregation in a corner or balcony. Any of these locations may be good, especially in situations where some question the desirability of a "special" choral ministry. Alternative positioning should be considered; however, if the choir is telling forth truth with a heart-intended ministry, they should speak as any other would. Most pastors do not preach from a balcony or corner nor do they face in a direction other than toward the people to whom they minister. The placement can and should reflect the philosophy of overall ministry of the local body.

"SOUND" ADVICE

Assuming a building is of sufficient size to require a sound-support system, it is very important to consider several factors. First and foremost it must be understood that the sound system is the *final link* between the platform and the congregation. All the training and preparation of all service participants, verbal and musical, must pass through the system before it reaches the people. The criteria for a sound support system include not only whether every one in the room can hear, but also the naturalness of the sound. The sound must not only be louder, it must be faithful: an accurate reflection of tone quality. It should sound just like the speaker or singer, only louder.

There are three basic links to the system, all of which must be of equally fine quality: the speaker(s), the microphone(s), and the amplifier/mixer control. All must represent the best available for the resources of a church body. It is not necessary to spend enormous sums for quality, but it is also senseless to waste money on ineffective, distorted equipment which is deemed good enough. Without becoming unduly technical we simply suggest that persons responsible for sound system selection purchase a compatible system which is as *flat* as possible. This means that the sound will be natural, treble or bass balancing with mid-sounds to afford maximum realism to the hearers. Knowledgeable sound advice is available in most communities. If possible, seek a resource person who can advise, and who does not represent a sales force; it is most difficult for a salesman to remain objective.

Good equipment does not guarantee good results if it is incorrectly installed or poorly operated. The primary speaker(s) for a meeting room should be located over the pulpit in most situations. This gives sound the best sense of direction, the best dispersion throughout the room, and the most even volume to the entire congregation. Speakers should be evaluated on the basis of their full frequency response and even sound dispersion. Generally, speakers should not be installed on the side walls or in the ceiling overhead. In the narthex, adjoining rooms, nurseries, etc., ceiling or wall-mounted speakers are fine.

Microphones must be carefully selected and correctly installed or they can prove to be the system's weak link. They should be chosen and placed as carefully as a photographer would choose his lens and focus it. There is no such thing as one microphone capable of meeting any application requirement. The microphone fixed on the pulpit should be shock-mounted so as to avoid a "thump" every time a book is dropped or something strikes the pulpit. Microphones over choirs must be a special type and be aimed toward the singers, not hung straight (perpendicular) to the floor. Only microphones currently in use should be on. To leave several on which are not in use increases unwanted noise and reduces the desirable signal. There are several other considerations with microphone quality and placement beyond the scope of this discussion, including lapel and wireless instruments which should be considered. Seek wise counsel.

Speakers and microphones can be of good quality, but if they are not connected to a proper amplifier with well-run controls they are for naught. The person(s) operating the sound for the local assembly should be located in the room which the sound services. It is unwise to place them in an isolated room or booth where they hear a monitor speaker. Operators should regulate volume on the basis of the same sound heard by the congregation. Attractive, lockable consoles are available which effectively house such equipment and render it most effective. The crew of persons responsible for sound must be dedicated, sensitive to balance, sensitive to the ministry needs of the body, patient, and available. They, like the equipment, can make or break all the hours of rehearsal and preparation if they fail in sound support.

A CONSIDERATION OF LIGHTING

Many rooms for worship are poorly lighted, to the conscious or unconscious frustration of all who attend. Lighting considerations go beyond simply whether people can see or not. Light adds life to an atmosphere when it is properly placed and used. Poorly placed or poorly controlled light can be most distracting. Light can add dramatic emphasis to events during a planned service—a sense of expectancy and anticipation. Dimming lights for certain times can help create a sense of quiet and introspection. An underlit building can actually be depressive in an evening service when all are looking for an "uplift" for the next day's opportunities.

Consider dimmable, selective lighting for the platform area which has enough intensity to affect daylight services. As one approaches the pulpit, raise the light on it so his arrival there and full light are simultaneous. The choir light should rise as the choir stands and dim as they are seated. This need not be an exotic, expensive system, especially in buildings which are smaller; but it can add so much. In large buildings regular theatrical lighting equipment is indicated. Many recent products designed to raise and lower lights throughout a residence can be applied to smaller situations. Of course, when dealing with electricity, proper care must be given to electrical loading; wires must be of proper size and local codes must be honored.

Lighting over the congregation should be bright enough for proper reading of hymnals and Bibles and should flood the entire room with enough light so that it feels bright without being hot or uncomfortable. Fluorescent (tube-type) lighting is convenient and less costly to operate, but it is not dimmable; it must either be on or off. This makes lighting transition very abrupt. Further, the type of light cast does not mix well with incandescent (bulb-type) light. It is not impossible to mix light types, but one must be well aware of the effectiveness and limitations of lighting.

Much more information about this important area is available through local sources.

Pulpits and Fences

Increasing emphasis on relationship and open communication today makes relevant some thought about our use of fixtures which seem to separate rather than to bring together. Occasionally one will enter a worship center where the piano is in one cage, the organ console in another (often widely separated), the choir has a cage, and the pastor stands behind the pulpit so his congregants wonder if he even has legs. This looks very neat and orderly but builds potential limitations.

There are the issues of modesty and the exhibition of shoe styles and bright socks, but the answer is not always partitions. Low, portable, flexible railings can be strategically placed in such a way as to enhance a feeling of open communication without isolation. If we avoid bolting railings to the floor, we open the possibilities for flexible seating and standing space for dramatic productions and visual creativity.

Many have reduced the size of the pulpit so it does not seem so awesome. Some have made the pulpit transparent so the entire person can be seen and still retain a place to stand and have a holder for Bible and notes. Beautiful furnishings are available which have a speaking top placed on the table used for communion. This reduces the amount of furniture and often brings the speaker and people closer together.

What About Instruments?

Many churches in the evangelical community have long settled on the notion that there are two acceptable instruments for music for our regular services, the piano and organ. We have already mentioned considerations for how these should be located, but what about the instruments themselves? What is a good piano or organ? A thorough discussion of that question would occupy volumes and still be open to preface and debate; but certain observations can be made.

It is important to consider excellent quality in an instrument purchase. To buy something deemed just good enough is often money poorly spent. Selection should be on the basis of the need and the proposed program utilization, not simply what can get us by. There are many fine pianos available. An instrument should be selected on the basis of tone quality, rugged reliable construction, and the right size for the room. It is wise for a church to first select a fine piano and perhaps wait on an organ purchase until such time as program and resources make it possible. (Why have two poor instruments?) Once purchased, it should be protected from extremes of humidity or temperature. A piano can suffer a great deal if it is not properly maintained, tuned twice yearly, and protected physically. It is safe to assume a grand piano is preferred to the upright, but in certain instances it may be wise to consider the relative merits of the other. A fine piano is a valuable, long-term investment for any church body. Giving it maximum attention, you can make wise use of this marvelous tool.

The instrument long associated with the church is the organ.

It is particularly well suited for hymn accompaniment, choir accompaniment, and service music from the first note of the prelude to the end of the postlude. For decades the only "real" organ for a church was considered to be a pipe organ; but given present day economics and late twentieth century electronics, the electronic organ must be seriously and musically considered. Some exciting work is being done combining pipes with electronics to give excellent results. Many builders (companies) are now providing fine, multitoned instruments with excellent chorus, ensemble, and solo stops.

The installation of the king of instruments is as important as the instrument itself. A fine organ, poorly installed, cannot do its best work. The location of the tonal opening(s) and its relationship to the room and the choir must be most carefully considered. A thoughtful committee should be charged with organ selection and recommendation. Various companies will provide volumes of information about their product. Of course, they will tell primarily of the virtues of their line. As with sound systems, serious seekers should find a consultant who has no financial attachment to the organ deal. As with the piano, an organ is a long term investment! It should be entered into very carefully with the total best interest of the church in mind. Sometimes spending more money is the wisest decision.

Many instruments other than the piano and organ are fitting for worship and service. It is always more a matter of heart than art, but artistic expression can surely be made on a variety of instruments. Many church bodies have formed instrumental ensembles, orchestras, and bands; may the trend continue! The magic world of electronics has perfected and provided many types of synthesizers—keyboard instruments producing sounds from string orchestras to brass bands and a lot more. They can glide from pitch to pitch, create spatial effects, or play very traditional melodies and harmonies. In the area of musical ministry, service comes in a variety of ways; let us be open to the possibilities. Choose not to be limited either by your imagination or traditions.

PARTING WORDS ON APPEARANCE

The environment for corporate worship has many ramifications, some of the most important of which we have briefly considered. The appearance of service participants is also important. It does not require that all must have just stepped off the page of a fashion magazine, but neat appearance and grooming should characterize Christ's servants. Neatly pressed shirts, some attention to color coordination, and platform etiquette should be assumed.

Appearance is not only in clothing and grooming. It includes attention to the proceedings. Have you ever seen platform people talking during a musical presentation or a choir member visiting during a message or Scripture reading? May God grant us a proper concept of manners, attention, and appearance. We reflect much of our concept of God and His people in these nonverbal ways.

Chapter 15

Conclusion:
So Let Us Celebrate

"We Sing the Greatness of Our God"

A celebration of heart does not come in an easy-open, prepared package. In these days of instant pudding and pop-top cans we have come to expect easy solutions, but heart worship is no prepackaged affair. This is not to say that heart worship is hopelessly difficult or that it is not worth pursuing. True worship is possible, it is God's will, and it is eminently worth pursuing!

The reactions to these chapters could be as varied as the character types of you who have read and thought with us. Some may say, "There really is not that much new here; we've been doing these kinds of things for years." Others may say, "These may be good ideas, but you simply do not know our church. Why, if we even changed the place in the order of worship where the DOXOLOGY is sung, the whole church would collapse!" Or, you might think that there are so many variations on this theme, that this book could simply be added to an already proliferating list. But wait; wherever you are in the adventure of worship, growth is possible and it is desirable. We will not know ultimate worship until we gather around the throne as a member of the great chorus of the redeemed of all the ages singing "Worthy is the Lamb . . . to receive honor and glory."

Some pastors who have read this far may have been trained

up to think that much of what has been said is another rehearsal of superfluous activity. "After all," they may say, "what really matters is the preaching; who cares about singing, environment, or art anyway?" Many have been influenced by the writing and statements of people like D. Martyn Lloyd-Jones in his "classic" for preachers where he says such things as:

> "I contend that we can lay it down as a fairly general rule that the greater the amount of attention that has been paid to this aspect of worship—namely the type of building, and the ceremonial, and the singing, and the music—the greater the emphasis on that, the less spirituality you are likely to have; and a lower spiritual temperature and spiritual understanding and desire can be expected."[1]

To make such a statement is unfortunately to confuse the matter of heart and art. If Satan can succeed in getting the people of God to discount or ignore the arts in expressing their love, adoration, and awe for God, he has robbed them of a very significant expressive and impressive force. God forbid that we should worship at the shrine of art, but may He likewise forbid the exclusion of art properly incorporated in the total work of ministry.

How Can We Grow?

Our strong suggestion for creating growth in the worship life of a local church is to involve as many as possible in the learning-planning process. Simply to secure a staff person and give them total responsibility to cultivate and enhance the worship life is to rob many of blessing and learning. (Sometimes adding staff to solve a church problem is an attempt to purchase a neat, packaged solution.)

Leadership should encourage broad congregational study into the Bible and helpful studies as those suggested in this work to enhance a spirit of discovery in worship. We must rid ourselves of our tendency toward spectatorism and traditionalism and become involved in the planning of meaningful, creative worship. Those who plan learn what to expect, and those who have high expectations of significant, dramatic encounter with God in worship are all more likely to experience it! At no point should we minimize Spirit-filled, biblical preaching; but how much more exciting it becomes when surrounded by heartfelt, artistic, participative activity.

Those who first see the light of meaningful change in their church's worship life must be sensitive to those for whom change is unsettling. To some there is great security in sameness, especially in these days of such insecurity and rapid change in the world at large. It has been well said that the seven last words of the church are "We never did it this way before!"

While change is often indicated and necessary, wholesale, insensitive change can be devastating. This is an area for much communication; help one another over hurdles with a spirit of love. Be committed to unity. If your church has been very staid and unemotional, do not force a great physical display. If the same order of service has been followed for decades, make small but well-explained changes with real meaning and gentleness. If your way of "doing it" has become redundant, lethargic, fake, overstated, understated, liturgical, disorganized, sloppy, stifled, etcetera, be willing prayerfully to seek worship which is full of spirit and truth. The truth frees (John 8:32); meaningless activity, no matter how "free" it may seem to be, is painfully restrictive and Spirit-quenching.

GOD, GRANT A HUNGER FOR CELEBRATION

In the contemplation of richer worship life, a group must move through prayer and studying and thinking together. Begin with small, attainable goals. Set out a plan to inform and motivate the people of God under your leadership to become more active seekers in worship. Our "me" generation with their "What's in it for me?" attitude must be led to a fuller mentality of worship by people more committed to God than to change. We must understand that getting anything *out* of worship depends directly on our willingness to put effort *in* to it!

May God grant to us a hunger for Him which will cause us to pursue Him in worship as a way of life (Colossians 3:17), a hunger which will drive us to closer fellowship with His people. This will result in a rich corporate worship experience, characterized by unity, sensitivity, and understanding (John 17). In loving God with our whole being we will love what He loves, hate what He hates, and long to see His purposes carried out through us! (Matthew 22:37)

Let us celebrate God!

Chapter 15, Notes

[1]D. Martyn Lloyd-Jones, *Preaching and Preachers* (Grand Rapids: Zondervan Publishers, 1972), p. 267.

Scripture Index

Subject Index

Bibliography
For Further Reading

Allen, Ronald Barclay. *Let Us Celebrate: A Call to Worship.* Portland, Or.: Western Conservative Baptist Seminary, 1981. (pamphlet)

_____. *Praise! A Matter of Life and Breath.* Nashville: Thomas Nelson Publishers, 1980.

Bailey, Robert W. *New Ways in Christian Worship.* Nashville: Broadman Press, 1981.

Dix, Dom Gregory. *The Shape of the Liturgy.* London: Adam & Charles Black, 1945.

Eskew, Harry; and Hugh T. McElrath. *Sing with Understanding.* Nashville: Broadman Press, 1980.

Fromm, Chuck. *Back to Basics: A Study of Public Music Ministry.* Costa Mesa: Ministry Resource Center, 1981. (pamphlet)

Gillquist, Peter E. *The Physical Side of Being Spiritual.* Grand Rapids: Zondervan Publishing House, 1979.

Hardin, Grady. *The Leadership of Worship.* Nashville: Abingdon, 1980.

Hodges, Zane C. *The Hungry Inherit Whetting Your Appetite for God.* 2nd ed. Portland, Or.. Multnomah Press. 1980.

Hustad, Donald P. *Jubilate! Church Music in the Evangelical Tradition.* Carol Stream, Ill.: Hope Publishing Company, 1980.

Kurtz, J. H. *Sacrificial Worship of the Old Testament.* Translated by James Martin. Reprint of 1863 ed. Grand Rapids: Baker Book House, 1980.

Leafblad, Bruce. *Music, Worship and the Ministry of the Church.* Portland, Or.: Western Seminary Press, 1977. (pamphlet)

Lovelace, Austin C.; and William C. Rice. *Music and Worship in the Church.* Rev. ed. Nashville: Abingdon, 1976.

Martin, Ralph P. *Worship in the Early Church.* Rev. Ed. Grand Rapids: Eerdmans, 1974.

Mitchell, Robert H. *Ministry and Music.* Philadelphia: The Westminster Press, 1978.

Ortlund, Anne. *Up With Worship.* Glendale: Regal Books, G/L Publishers, 1975.

Rayburn, Robert G. *O Come, Let Us Worship: Corporate Worship in the Evangelical Church.* Grand Rapids: Baker Book House, 1980.

Reynolds, William J. *Congregational Singing.* Nashville: Convention Press, 1975.

_____. *A Joyful Sound: Christian Hymnody.* 2nd ed., prepared by Milburn Price. New York: Holt, Reinhart and Winston, 1978.

Rookmaaker, H. R. *Art Needs No Justification.* Downers Grove, Ill.: Inter-Varsity Press, 1978. (pamphlet)

Schaeffer, Franky. *Addicted to Mediocrity*. Westchester, Ill.: Crossway Books, 1981.

Toon, Peter. *Knowing God Through the Liturgy*. Bramcote, Notts., Great Britain: Grove Books, 1974.

Tozer, A. W. *Worship: The Missing Jewel of the Evangelical Church*. Harrisburg, Pa.: Christian Publications, Inc., [n.d.]. (pamphlet)

Unruh, Wilfred J. *Planning Congregational Worship*. Worship Series No. 2. Rev. Ed. Scottdale, Pa.: Mennonite Publishing House, 1979. (pamphlet)

Webber, Robert E. *Common Roots: A Call to Evangelical Maturity*. Grand Rapids: Zondervan Publishing House, 1978.

White, James F. *New Forms of Worship*. Nashville: Abingdon Press, 1971.

Willimon, William H. *Word, Water, Wine and Bread: How Worship Has Changed Over the Years*. Valley Forge: Judson Press, 1980.

Wilson, John F. *An Introduction to Church Music*. Chicago: Moody Press, 1965.

Wohlgemuth, Paul W. *Rethinking Church Music*. Rev. Ed. Carol Stream, Ill.: Hope Publishing Company, 1981.

Books in the Critical Concern series:
- ABORTION: Toward An Evangelical Consensus, Paul Fowler
- BEYOND HUNGER: A Biblical Mandate for Social Responsibility, Art Beals, Larry Libby
- BIRTHRIGHT: Christian, Do You Know Who You Are?, David Needham
- CHRISTIAN COUNTERMOVES IN A DECADENT CULTURE, Carl F. H. Henry
- THE CHRISTIAN MINDSET IN A SECULAR SOCIETY: Promoting Evangelical Renewal and National Righteousness, Carl F. H. Henry
- THE CHRISTIAN, THE ARTS, AND TRUTH: Regaining the Vision of Greatness, Frank Gaebelein, D. Bruce Lockerbie
- CHRISTIANS IN THE WAKE OF THE SEXUAL REVOLUTION: Recovering Our Sexual Sanity, Randy Alcorn
- THE CONTROVERSY: Roots of the Creation-Evolution Conflict, Donald Chittick
- THE COSMIC CENTER: The Supremacy of Christ in a Secular Wasteland, D. Bruce Lockerbie
- CULTURE IN CHRISTIAN PERSPECTIVE: A Door to Understanding and Enjoying the Arts, Leland Ryken
- DECISION MAKING AND THE WILL OF GOD: A Biblical Alternative to the Traditional View, Garry Friesen, J. Robin Maxson
- DEPRESSION: Finding Hope & Meaning in Life's Darkest Shadow, Don Baker, Emery Nester
- EUTHANASIA: Spiritual, Medical & Legal Issues in Terminal Health Care, Beth Spring, Ed Larson
- IMAGINATION: Embracing a Theology of Wonder, Cheryl Forbes
- A JUST DEFENSE: The Use of Force, Nuclear Weapons & Our Conscience, Karl Payne, Keith Payne
- LIBERATED TRADITIONALISM: Men & Women in Balance, Ronald & Beverly Allen
- LIFE-STYLE EVANGELISM: Crossing Traditional Boundaries to Reach the Unbelieving World, Joseph Aldrich
- THE MAJESTY OF MAN: The Dignity of Being Human, Ronald B. Allen
- THE TRAUMA OF TRANSPARENCY: A Biblical Approach to Inter-personal Communication, J. Grant Howard
- WORSHIP: Rediscovering the Missing Jewel, Ronald B. Allen, Gordon Borror